COASTAL HARVEST

COASTAL HARVEST

FISH · FORAGE · FEAST   TAKU KONDO

DK

Publisher Mike Sanders
Art & Design Director William Thomas
Editorial Director Ann Barton
Executive Editor Alexander Rigby
Designer Lindsay Dobbs
Illustrator Dwight Hwang
Photographer Jocelyn Gonzalez
Recipe Tester Bee Berrie
Development Editor Tiffany Taing
Copyeditor Cindy Nguyen-Pham
Proofreaders Mira Park, Lisa Starnes
Indexer Beverlee Day

First American Edition, 2025
Published in the United States by DK Publishing
1745 Broadway, 20th Floor, New York, NY 10019

The authorized representative in the EEA is Dorling Kindersley
Verlag GmbH. Arnulfstr. 124, 80636 Munich, Germany

Copyright © 2025 by Taku Kondo
DK, a Division of Penguin Random House LLC
25 26 27 28 29 10 9 8 7 6 5 4 3 2 1
001-339819-MAR2025

Library of Congress Catalog Number: 2024947296
ISBN 978-0-7440-9457-2

DK books are available at special discounts when purchased
in bulk for sales promotions, premiums, fundraising, or
educational use. For details, contact SpecialSales@dk.com

Printed and bound in China

Photographs on pages 15, 16, 17, 28, and 99 by Shayla Penera

www.dk.com

MIX
Paper | Supporting
responsible forestry
FSC™ C018179

This book was made with Forest
Stewardship Council™ certified
paper – one small step in DK's
commitment to a sustainable future.
Learn more at
www.dk.com/uk/information/sustainability

*To all the people on YouTube who
have asked if I have a cookbook.
The answer is finally yes!*

CONTENTS

SHELLFISH

COASTAL PLANTS

WILD MUSHROOMS

Introduction

My love for the outdoors and my passion for food have led me to live the life I have today. I was born in Osaka, also known as the food capital of Japan. I've been eating delicious food ever since I was a child, and those memories and flavors are forever ingrained in me. My mother is the biggest influence in my life, not only for my love of cooking but also for the way I live. I moved to the United States with my mother and two brothers at the age of nine. When you're a kid, you just go along with whatever your parents tell you. So my brothers and I started going to school in the US without knowing any English, and we assimilated to the culture partly by watching television. Years later, when I was close to twenty years old, I thought about how I never really knew the reason why we moved to the US in the first place. So I asked her about it, and she replied, "So you guys could play and be kids." She explained how the life of a child in Japan involves an incredible amount of studying and extracurricular activities in order to ensure success later in life. Quite the opposite of the stereotypical Asian parent, she wanted us to be able to enjoy our time as kids instead of stressing over academics. This mindset of enjoying life has propelled me to make life choices that prioritize enjoyment, passion, and love.

When I was a kid, you'd hardly catch me inside. I was usually out playing sports, fishing, making bows and arrows, riding bikes, and a lot more. As I was obsessed with the outdoors, my father introduced me to fishing at the age of five. He'd take us out on weekend camping and fishing trips in Japan, and I absolutely loved it. My father never moved to the US with us because he was unable to obtain a visa. The plan was for my dad to stay an extra year in Japan to help support us financially while we got settled in. Right around the time he was planning to move to the US, 9/11 happened. US immigration shut down, and it became impossible to attain a visa, even with the help of lawyers. He stayed in Japan and would come visit us once a year for about a week or two, during which we always had some fishing and camping planned.

I went on to study kinesiology at San Francisco State University in the hopes of becoming a physical therapist. However, I had always enjoyed cooking with my mom, so in between my studies, I continued growing as a home cook. In my last month of completing my degree, I decided to try cooking in a professional kitchen. I thought I was pretty badass at home, so I wanted to test my skills against the pros. I was immediately humbled when they asked me to bring my knives with me. As I pulled out my $3 Daiso knife from under the counter, the chef intercepted and put it right back. He said, "You can borrow one of my knives," and from there, the training began. This was in a high-end Japanese restaurant in San Francisco that served wagyu and sushi. I wanted to understand the sushi side of things to get back to my roots. I've always enjoyed the fine knife work demonstrated by sushi chefs. In no time, I learned how to prepare all the vegetables and how to make maki-zushi (rolls). I learned fast and worked hard to gain the skills I needed to be part of the actual sushi bar, but the maki station was in the open kitchen, away from customers and in the background. To make a long story short, after working my butt off for a year, I still wasn't promoted to the sushi bar. I quit the restaurant to put my kinesiology degree to use by working in an outpatient physical therapy clinic. I enjoyed my time

there—I had weekends and holidays off, and it was a laid-back atmosphere, but there was just something about pursuing cooking as a career that felt more passionate and rewarding. So, after a year working in physical therapy, I went back to work in the same restaurant as before for round two.

There were several months of overlap working both jobs, but this time, I was promised a spot at the sushi bar. I gained even more skills: fileting all kinds of fish, slicing sashimi, and making nigiri. I worked my way up and kept learning everything I could. I was on my way to quickly becoming one of the senior chefs, but when I started teaching more than I was actively learning, I knew it was time for me to go once more. It wasn't that I didn't want to teach the new guys but rather that I felt I needed to train more myself before I could do so. I went to work for an omakase-style sushi restaurant in SF to get more experience in the trade. That's where I refined my skills and focused more on the details.

The one thing missing from my life as a sushi chef was the outdoors, so I decided to create my YouTube channel, Outdoor Chef Life, to combine my two passions. I soon became obsessed with catching and harvesting items to put into my dishes because it's a chef's dream to work with the freshest ingredients. In the beginning, my bread and butter was coastal foraging. It requires minimal tools: a bucket, a pocketknife, and gloves will do most of the time. In college, I randomly picked up a book called *The Bay Area Forager* by Kevin Feinstein and Mia Andler, which taught me how to identify and harvest a lot of plants local to me. Once I realized there was protein available on the coast, I was hooked. I started teaching myself about the intertidal zone from books like *The Sea Forager's Guide to the Northern California Coast* by Kirk Lombard and *Between Pacific Tides* by Edward F. Ricketts and Jack Calvin, applying my newfound knowledge in my YouTube videos to make fresh, local, and creative dishes.

This book is not about one topic but rather, many. Not only will you learn about making sushi and fileting fish, but you'll also read about fishing, foraging, and identifying plants and mushrooms. The recipes included in this book are inspired both by my restaurant work and by original recipes and techniques I've developed over the years. I also talk about sustainability as well as utilizing all parts of the fish. You get the prized filets, and you also get to experiment with underutilized portions like the guts, roe, or fins. The highlight of harvesting your own fish is that creative possibilities are endless. I hope to inspire you to harvest your own fish or, if you already do, I hope you can learn from these recipes to deepen your connection to the food you eat and fully appreciate your catch.

FOUNDATIONS

Knife Basics

Sushi chefs have some of the finest knife skills in the culinary world. These skills don't come without practice, and the key is to practice the proper technique. Cutting fast is cool, and looking away while cutting fast is even cooler, but if the cuts aren't consistent, you're going to get sent home. All right, all right—if you're doing it at home, that consequence doesn't matter as much, but in restaurants, chefs will take one look at your work and tell you to start over. True story, my first week at the restaurant, I cut green onions for sushi. I was told to cut them thin, so that's what I did. Or at least, that's what I thought I did. As soon as the chef looked at my work, he told me to take it to the hotline for miso soup because it was too thick. I thought he was joking at first, but it turns out he was dead serious. The level of precision required to be a sushi chef is no joke. Before getting into technique, let's get to know the different styles of knives.

Japanese Gyuto Knives vs. Western Chef's Knives

There are several key differences between these two types of knives. Western knives are always made with stainless steel, whereas Japanese knives are made with high-carbon steel. The difference is the hardness of the steel. Stainless is softer, while carbon is harder. They both have their advantages and disadvantages. Stainless is less likely to chip and damage when cutting through harder foods, but it dulls faster and doesn't get as sharp. It's also easier to maintain. Carbon can get extremely sharp and hold edges longer (meaning they stay sharp), but it's more brittle, making it likelier to chip the blade if it hits a hard object—for example, cutting through bones or frozen food. It also takes more maintenance, as carbon steel will oxidize and rust. One way to avoid the rust is to keep the knife dry, wiping the blade with a dry towel every time you are about to put it down.

Besides the blade material, the other major difference between these two styles of knives is the shape of the blade. Western chef's knives provide more of a curved edge through the entire blade, whereas gyuto knives, aka Japanese chef's knives, have a straighter or flatter edge that curves only toward the tip. Why is this important? These differences will affect the way you cut. Western chef's knives are more useful for rocking styles of cutting. Gyuto knives are more useful in push and pull cuts.

Another difference is the thickness of the blade. Gyuto knives are thinner, making it easier to slice through dense vegetables like carrots and potatoes.

Gyuto knives are all double-bevel, similar to other chef's knives and all Western knives. A double-bevel knife is sharpened on both sides of the blade. A lot of Japanese knives are single-bevel, meaning they are sharpened only on one side and the other side remains flat. The advantage of a single-bevel has to do with the sharpness of the blade.

Types of Knives

Chef's knife: The most versatile type of knife. Its uses include preparing vegetables, cutting meat, and fileting fish.

Recommended blade length: 8 to 10 inches (21 to 27cm).

Gyuto: An all-around knife and highly versatile. Its uses include preparing vegetables, cutting meat, slicing sashimi, and fileting fish (though take care not to cut through the bones).

Recommended blade length: 8 to 9 ½ inches (21 to 24cm).

Filet knife: Thin and flexible knife. Used for cleaning and fileting fish.

Recommended blade length: 8 to 9 ½ inches (21 to 24cm).

Deba: The Japanese filet knife but with a completely different take. This single-bevel knife is extremely thick and heavy compared other knives. I consider it to be the workhorse of knives, as I can do just about anything with it. Its uses include cleaning and fileting fish, but it is not good for slicing sashimi due to its short and stout shape.

Recommended blade length: 6 to 8 inches (15 to 21cm).

Nakiri: Rectangular-shaped knife popular for home cooks who prepare many vegetables. The advantage is its ability to scoop up what you cut in a single motion.

Recommended blade length: 6 ½ to 7 ½ inches (16.5 to 19cm).

Yanagiba: Very long, single-bevel knife specifically used for slicing sashimi. If you plan on preparing a lot of raw fish, this knife is a must-have in your bag. It is usually the sharpest knife in the arsenal.

Recommended blade length: 9 ½ to 12 inches (24 to 30cm).

Bunka: Similar to the gyuto, the bunka is a multipurpose knife with a pointed tip for fine slicing (i.e., thin cuts of avocado). The smaller surface area on the tip lends to less friction, which allows for smooth and accurate cutting. A great knife for both home cooks and professionals.

Recommended blade length: 7 ½ to 9 ½ inches (19 to 24cm).

Santoku: A knife that lies between a nakiri and a gyuto. It is also a multipurpose knife popular with home cooks. Its uses include cutting vegetables, meat, and fish (not fileting).

Recommended blade length: 6 ½ to 7 inches (16.5 to 18cm).

Petty or paring knife: Short and small knife great for fine-detail work. Its uses include peeling, paring, and cutting small sections, like apple cores or potato studs.

Recommended blade length: 4 ½ to 6 inches (11.5 to 15cm).

What are my top three knives? If I could only bring three knives with me, I would choose a 9 ½-inch (24cm) gyuto, a 12-inch (30cm) yanagiba, and a 7-inch (18cm) deba.

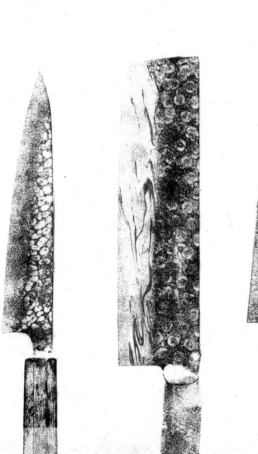

Cutting Techniques

There are several different methods of cutting. Push cuts, pull cuts, and rocking cuts are the most common techniques. With these cutting skills, you can master preparing all kinds of ingredients. Knife grip is very important when it comes to proper technique. Holding the knife correctly in your hand will give you the best control and leverage. The most common grip you'll use is the pinch grip. Hold the knife in your dominant hand and balance the face of the blade on your index finger, which should be about an inch forward from the top of the handle. With your index finger and thumb, pinch the back of the blade and wrap your other fingers around the handle. Another common grip I often use is the finger on top. It's similar to the pinch grip, except the index finger goes on the spine of the blade. This grip gives you more control and precision, and I like to use it when I'm slicing for sashimi and sushi. Here are three popular cutting techniques and when to use them.

Push cut: This is what I use on most vegetables. With the push-cut method, the knife is pushed down and forward simultaneously. Your wrist should be locked in position, and the motion should come from your arm and shoulder. The forward motion allows the knife to slice through the object with ease, as opposed to pushing through it. Knives are most effective when there is a slicing motion involved. The phrase "Let the knife do the work" applies here. You'll be able to achieve the thinnest slices of green onion with this cutting technique. Use this method with gyuto, bunka, and nakiri knives.

Pull cut: This is very similar to the push cut. Instead of pushing down and forward, you pull down and back. It's a very unnatural motion for most people and requires practice. You can achieve very thin slices with this technique. The biggest advantage of the pull cut is that it preserves the knife edge because you're only lightly tapping the blade against the cutting surface, meaning your knife will stay sharp longer. Use this method with gyuto, bunka, and nakiri knives.

Rocking: This method is the most common in Western cuisine. Start with the tip of the knife down on the cutting board, and rock the entire length of the blade. Rocking ensures that the object is cut all the way through. The disadvantage of this technique is that the motion comes from the wrist. If you're doing a lot of prep work, this may be strenuous on your wrist over time. Use this method with chef and santoku knives.

Cutting Boards

The cutting board is an underrated tool in the kitchen. Cutting surfaces affect cutting performance. If you're going to use a nice and expensive knife, make sure to invest in a good-quality cutting board.

Bamboo is eco-friendly and has become one of the most common types of cutting boards. The hard surface makes it less absorbent and therefore more resistant to bacterial growth, but it's one of the worst for your knife edge. If you use a bamboo cutting board, it doesn't matter how sharp your knife is—it'll soon dull. So, what cutting boards should you use instead?

Hi-Soft cutting boards are what the majority of sushi restaurants use and are my favorite choice. These boards are made from a soft, dense synthetic rubber material that allows the knife to make contact with the board with minimal dulling to the knife edge. They last for years without warping and are easy to clean. Hi-Soft cutting boards can be used to cut everything from raw meats to vegetables, and they're the best board to use with high-carbon knives, like Japanese knives. Plus, they just feel good to cut on!

Wood cutting boards are beautiful and multifunctional. They're great for cutting as well as plating charcuterie or sushi, and they're softer than bamboo cutting boards, making them better for the knife edge. Wood boards are also naturally antibacterial, making them much safer to use than plastic boards. Look for woods like maple, walnut, cherry, or hinoki. End-grain boards have a checkerboard pattern and are very good surfaces for knife-edge retention. Long-grain boards have horizontal lines. They have the advantage of being less expensive than end-grain boards, but they are not as good at retaining the knife edge. Wood boards should be dried after washing and regularly oiled.

Plastic cutting boards are the cheapest option, and the best thing about them is that they are lightweight, which makes them easy to pack for camping and outdoor cooking. Most are also dishwasher safe, though plastic may warp when in contact with heat.

Knife Sharpening

Having a sharp knife is one of the key aspects to cutting better, more consistently, and more precisely. The importance of a sharp knife is not to be taken lightly. There's a reason why I take my own knives with me anywhere I go. I keep my knives well maintained at maximum sharpness so they always offer a clean cut.

How often should I sharpen my knives?

This is a very common question I get. It definitely depends on how often you use them, but it also depends on what you're cutting and the cutting surface you're using. Instead of me saying to sharpen your knives every five or ten uses, it's best to understand the cutting performance of your knife. First, if you have a knife you've been using for years that has never been sharpened, the best thing to do is to send it to a professional to sharpen it.

Next, let's talk about a new knife you've recently acquired and how and when to sharpen it. A new knife out of the box should already be very sharp and shouldn't need additional sharpening before first use. You can try running some tests to figure out its baseline sharpness. For instance, try slicing a piece of paper, test out how thinly you can slice a green onion or see how easy it is to cut through a tomato. Make a mental note of the knife's performance. After about a week of regular use, run the same tests again. If the knife doesn't perform as well as it did when you first bought and used it, you need to sharpen it. If it performs the same, keep using it as is. A month is the longest I would go without sharpening my knives. Keep in mind that it's easier and quicker to achieve sharpness the more frequently you sharpen. It will take more effort to bring back the sharp edge the longer you let it dull.

Why is a sharp knife important to have?

The first and most important reason is for safety. A dull knife requires more force to cut, which makes it easy for the knife to slip and potentially cut you. Another reason is efficiency. Properly sharpened knives require less force to cut through ingredients and will save you time and effort, making your job of cutting much easier and more enjoyable. A sharp knife is able to cut with precision, control, and consistency. These are all important aspects, especially when working with delicate ingredients like fish.

What do I use to sharpen my knives?

The best way to sharpen your knives is with a whetstone, which is a block made of natural or artificial materials of different grit. The higher the grit count, the finer the material. I recommend having three whetstones of varying grit counts: 300 to 600 grit, 1000 to 1200 grit, and 3000 to 6000 grit. If you're just starting out and want to get one to start with, choose a 1000 to 1200 grit.

I do most of my regular sharpening on 1000- to 1200-grit stones in less than five minutes. Assuming that you're sharpening a new knife, this grit stone is the perfect place to start as you can achieve the same out-of-the-box sharpness. For an even sharper edge, finish the sharpening with a 3000- to 6000-grit stone. The 300- to 600-grit stone is for when you've let your knife dull a bit more than usual or when you need to fix a chip in the knife. That level of grit pulls more material off, making it a faster process for fixing knives.

Steel honing rods are used for honing rather than sharpening. Using a knife creates microscopic bends in the edge. Honing will straighten those bends out, allowing the knives to perform better. This technique is most commonly used with stainless steel knives. Be very careful when using a honing steel on a carbon knife as it can chip the knife if used incorrectly—meaning, don't try to be cool and do the Gordon Ramsay thing with your Japanese knives. Honing rods do not remove any material, so you should still sharpen your knives with a whetstone.

Ceramic honing rods are another option for sharpening. Ceramic will actually remove material and can be used in between regular sharpenings.

How do I sharpen my knives?

Most whetstones need to be soaked in cold water for fifteen minutes before use. Make sure the stone is firmly in place. (You can use a small, damp towel for this.) Start with the tip of the knife on the center of the whetstone. Lightly place your index and middle fingers on the side of the knife blade. The opposing knife edge should be held at roughly a 15-degree angle relative to the stone. Use an up-and-down sliding motion to guide the knife over the whetstone ten times for each set, and repeat on every inch of the blade. Note that you are only sharpening the part where your fingers are applying pressure. Keeping that in mind, move your fingers down the knife slightly with each set. You will start to notice residue forming on the stone. This "mud" is the mix of ceramic from the whetstone and the steel from your knife. Do not wipe this off as it helps to sharpen the knife. After you've gone through the entire knife, check on the other side for a burr, which is when the knife edge curls to the opposite side of the sharpened edge. Once a burr is achieved, move on to the other side of the knife, repeating the same steps. Repeating the entire process two to three times is enough for regularly sharpened knives. To get rid of the burr, start with the tip of the knife and gently run the entire edge against the stone. Do this five to ten times on one side and then again on the other. Now, alternate the same motion from one side to the other. Your knife is ready to go.

Scan for bonus content.

Cleaning and Fileting Fish

How to Clean Fish

Before you filet any fish, the first step is to scale and gut it. I'm often asked why you need to scale the fish, and there are many reasons. Scaling fish allows a knife to cut through the skin with ease and precision, making it safer and less prone to accidents. It keeps the work area and cutting board clean. Fileting an unscaled fish makes a mess, and scales can end up on the cutting board, the knife, the fish, and the final dish. If you're making sushi, that's a big no-no. Scales also keep moisture in the fish, which can be a breeding ground for bacteria. Once a fish is scaled, the slime will be removed as well, keeping the work surface cleaner and helping to avoid cross contamination. Lastly, the skin is edible, but the scales are not (unless fried). Scaling the fish opens up the possibilities for what you can make with it and how you can cook it.

There are different tools you can use to scale fish. A scaler is the best tool for fish with large scales, like sea bass, snapper, and grouper. Simply start at the tail and scrape the scales from tail to head. This will remove the scales from most fish. However, scalers don't work as effectively on fish with smaller scales, such as halibut, yellowtail, and mahi mahi. For these fish, a stainless steel sponge brush works much better. Alternatively, there is a Japanese scaling method called sukibiki, where scaling is done using a sharp knife: rather than scraping the scales, the scales are gently sliced off the fish. The thought behind this method is that fish have delicate flesh, and aggressively scaling it can tear the meat. The sukibiki technique is gentler on the flesh, ensuring a high-quality fish filet. This is one of the many details that sushi chefs focus on to make the best sushi.

To remove the guts and gills of the fish, insert a knife into the anus on the underside of the fish and cut all the way to the gills. Use shears or a knife to disconnect the gills toward the top of the head as well as by the throat. The membrane between the gills and the collar also needs to be cut. Grab ahold of the gills and pull downward. The guts and gills will come out all together. Use a knife to scrape the inside cavity on the underside of the spine. This bloodline is the fish's kidneys. Run it under cold water to wash away. Pat dry, and the fish is ready for fileting.

How to Filet Fish

There are multiple ways to filet fish, but as a sushi chef, I recommend two main methods: sanmai oroshi (three-piece breakdown) and gomai oroshi (five-piece breakdown). The three-piece is the most common way to filet fish and takes its name from the three pieces at the end of the fish: the two filets and the carcass. This method is typically used to filet most fish, including salmon, sea bass, and snapper. The five-piece breakdown is used to filet fish like tuna or halibut and provides you with five pieces: the top loin and bottom loin from both filets, plus the carcass.

Fileting fish can be a delicate process that requires skill and care to do safely. Here are some safety tips to keep in mind:

- **Use the right tools.** A sharp knife and a cutting board with a nonslip surface are essential. Dull knives can slip and cause accidents. I prefer using a big chef's knife over filet knives to filet fish. Chef's knives have a stronger backbone and are able to easily get through bones. A lot of filet knives are too flimsy in my opinion. I don't need a bendable knife to filet fish, but this amounts to personal preference. Most Japanese chefs use a deba knife to filet fish. They are great knives to get the job done, but I think the thickness makes it more difficult to feel the bones. So a chef's knife is right in between the two.

- **Maintain a stable work area.** Make sure your cutting surface is clean, stable, and at a comfortable working height. Cutting on an uneven surface will increase the difficulty level as well as the risk of an accident.

- **Start with a secure grip.** Hold the fish firmly by the tail, and keep your fingers clear of the cutting area.

- **Position yourself correctly.** Stand in a comfortable position, work with good lighting, and ensure you have a clear view of what you're doing.

- **Follow the natural contours.** Use the natural shape of the fish's bones and body as a guide.

- **Angle the knife.** Angle the knife slightly toward the bones to minimize waste and ensure a smooth cut.

- **Use controlled, even strokes.** Apply gentle, controlled pressure, and use long, smooth strokes rather than sawing motions.

- **Watch your fingers.** Keep your fingers tucked in and away from the knife blade.

- **Work slowly and steadily.** Take your time, especially if you're a beginner. Rushing increases the chance of accidents.

- **Clean as you go.** Always have a small, damp towel to wipe your knife and cutting board with. Avoid cutting on slippery work surfaces to prevent accidents.

- **Use a towel or cloth for gripping.** If the fish is particularly slippery, you can use a clean towel or cloth to improve your grip.

- **Practice good hygiene.** Wash your hands thoroughly before and after handling fish, and clean all equipment after use.

Scan for bonus content.

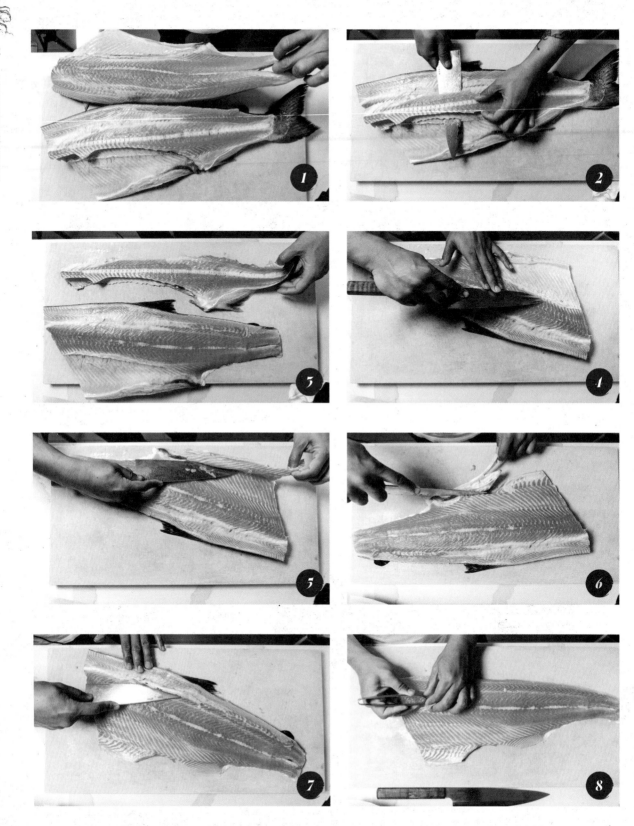

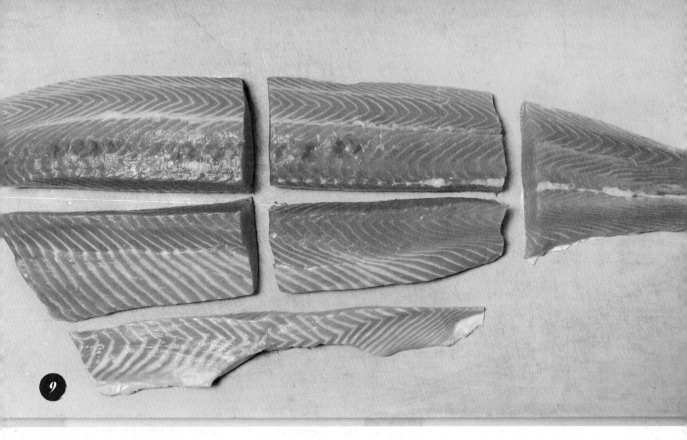

9

Preparing Fish for Sashimi

The care for fish used in sashimi dishes starts as soon as the fish hits the deck of a fishing boat, where it is immediately dispatched by a Japanese method called ike jime. When a fish is caught, it uses all its energy to thrash around. The longer the fish thrashes, the more lactic acid is released into the meat and the higher the temperature of the meat rises. The sooner you can put the fish out of its misery, the better the quality of meat will be. So with the ike jime method, a sharp point is used to swiftly penetrate the fish's brain. Dispatching a fish quickly is the most humane way to respectfully end its life. Then the gills are cut and, depending on the size, the tail is also cut to help bleed the fish quicker. Blood left in a fish can will cause it to go bad quickly, while fish that has been bled out will last much longer and remain fresher over time.

When a commercial fish from Japan is transported, there is an agreement among fishmongers and chefs that the fish will always rest on its right side during packaging and shipping. This ensures that there is always a filet with top-quality meat because the left side of the fish experiences less weight and pressure. You can see this practiced in many fish markets, as they lay the fish down on its right side and show you the left side of the fish.

There are three proper ways to hold a whole fish. You can hold it vertically with one hand with your thumb and finger in the eye socket of the fish. You can also hold the fish with two hands to support its entire weight. Or you can hold it vertically by the tail. These techniques ensure that the fish's meat will not break apart during handling. Fish meat is very delicate and easily ruined by rough handling. Similarly, never bend a fish filet; instead, always support the entire weight with two hands or hold it up vertically. These small details help produce the finest end result for sashimi.

Scan for bonus content.

Storing Fish

In the Refrigerator

Storing the fish whole keeps it fresher longer (if it's not being frozen). Make salt water as salty as the ocean (meaning about 3 percent salt) in a container large enough to submerge the fish. Place the cleaned fish in the salt water for a few minutes. Then pat dry as much as you can, place a clean paper towel in the gut cavity to soak up any blood that may leak out when stored, and wrap the fish in parchment paper or plastic wrap. Whole fish will keep in the refrigerator for up to a week, but be sure to change the paper towels and parchment daily. Use this method for small and medium fish like sardines, mackerel, snapper, flounder, etc.

Once you filet the fish, avoid washing it with fresh water. If the fish was properly scaled, gutted, and cleaned before fileting, there's likely no need to wash the filets (another benefit of scaling). Washing filets can change the texture and also potentially create an environment for bacteria growth, as mentioned earlier. When storing filets, make sure to pat dry any moisture and wrap individual filets with a paper towel and then plastic wrap. Fish filets will keep in the fridge for up to three days. Change paper towels daily.

In the Freezer

The most common method for sport fishermen is to freeze fish that will not be consumed immediately. Doing so kills parasites, making it safer to eat raw. To freeze fish after fileting, I recommend keeping the skin on. I like to cut portions that I'll eat in a single meal and vacuum seal those portions before freezing. Make sure there is minimal moisture on the filets. Write the date and species on the bag with a permanent marker. Kept frozen, fish will be safe and good in raw preparations for several months. White fish like snapper and halibut tend to not freeze very well. The texture becomes watery and mushy, making it not as tasty for sashimi. Fish like tuna and salmon freeze very well, meaning the texture changes minimally, which makes them great for sashimi or sushi even after being frozen for months. Use your best judgment when preparing fish that has been frozen for an extended period. Smell is very important; if it smells off, it's not good for any raw preparation. In these cases, cook the fish. With tuna, the color will become darker over time. As long as it's a darker red and not brown, it will be good for sushi. Restaurants keep tuna colder than most home freezers, which keeps the color more vibrant for longer.

To defrost fish, transfer it from the freezer to the refrigerator the day before use, or submerge it in cold water for 30 minutes to an hour or until defrosted. Do not place the filet directly in the water; instead, make sure it's in a sealed plastic bag. Once defrosted, pat dry excess moisture and keep wrapped with a paper towel and plastic wrap in the fridge.

Sushi

As a sushi chef, it's only right that I include detailed techniques on how to make the best sushi at home. First, we need to know what sushi is.

What Is Sushi?

Contrary to popular belief, sushi is not characterized by raw fish. Sushi means "vinegar rice" in Japanese. Although vinegar rice is often paired with raw fish, it is not a requirement. In fact, you can make sushi with cooked fish. There are traditional preparations of sushi using cooked ingredients instead of raw, like unagi (grilled eel) sushi. So, when people ask what the most important part of sushi is, it's definitely the rice. Sashimi, however, strictly refers to raw fish. Sashimi does not contain any rice.

Types of Sushi

Maki (rolls): The most common type of sushi anywhere in the world. There are two types: regular maki (aka hosomaki), which has seaweed on the outside, and uramaki, which has rice on the outside. Uramaki is more common in the Western world than in Japan and often includes sauces and nontraditional ingredients.

Nigiri: Traditional bite-size sushi that has a small piece of fish, usually raw, over rice. Nigiri looks very simple, but it's the most difficult to master.

Chirashi: Bowl of sushi rice topped with various fish and vegetables. This is the easiest type of sushi to make, as it doesn't require rolling or nigiri.

Temaki: Also known as hand rolls. Temaki uses half a sheet of nori (seaweed) with rice and fish and is rolled into a cone by hand. Hand rolls are easy to prepare and are often the type of sushi made in Japanese households. When I was growing up, my family had "hand roll nights," when the sushi rice and all the other ingredients were laid out, and each person could make their own hand roll with their preferred choice of fillings and toppings as we sat around the dining table.

Sashimi: Raw fish that's eaten without rice but with soy sauce and wasabi. It is the simplest-looking piece of raw fish created with the most amount of care and precision. Sashimi can be rather expensive because of the care required to prepare the fish.

Sushi Lessons and Techniques

Portioning salmon for sushi

Portion the fish into 6-inch (15cm) blocks for sashimi and nigiri. In sushi terms, the cut is called *saku*. These saku blocks of fish will give you the best results for making any kind of sushi. A salmon filet is typically portioned into six pieces: the belly portion, two lower portions, two upper portions, and one tail portion. Make sure to freeze all wild salmon before consuming raw.

Portioning tuna for sushi

Cut 6-inch (15cm) saku blocks from a tuna filet. Portions closest to the skin with a heavy concentration of sinew (the white connective tissue that runs in the tuna meat) should be scraped off using a spoon to separate the meat from the sinew. Sinew is edible but chewy when concentrated. All of the tuna scraps and trimmings can be made into rolls like spicy tuna and tartare.

Scan for bonus content.

Portioning white fish (halibut, sea bass, snapper, etc.) for sushi

Remove the middle section where the pin bones run, and separate the filet into two sections: the belly and the shoulder. This goes for most fish.

Scan for bonus content.

Portioning baitfish or hikarimono (mackerel, sardines, gizzard shad, etc.) for sushi

These smaller fish require different portioning methods. The entire filet is used as one saku block, which means it is necessary to remove all pin bones in the filets with tweezers. There are special pin bone tweezers for this job, but if they are not available to you, pliers will work well as an alternative. Make sure to sanitize any tools that will be used for this job. Generally, the fresher the fish, the more difficult it is to remove the pin bones. Fresh fish tend to be tense and hold on to the pin bones. By letting the fish sit for a day, the job will become a lot easier.

Scan for bonus content.

How to Make Sushi

When making sushi, position all ingredients and tools within reach. You will need the following:

- **Small bowl of cold water** for dipping your hands into. This helps to prevent the rice from getting stuck all over your hands. If you're finding the rice too sticky, try using ice water instead or add a small drop of neutral oil to the water.

- **Cutting board** to prepare sushi on and to cut the rolls.

- **Sharp knife,** like a gyuto or chef's knife for precision slicing.

- **Makisu (rolling mat)** to shape the rolls. To make uramaki (rice on the outside), wrap the rolling mat in plastic wrap to prevent the rice from sticking to the mat. When making rolls with seaweed on the outside, plastic wrap is not necessary.

- **Sushi rice** set off to the side in a large bowl or container with a clean, damp towel on top to prevent the rice from drying out.

- **Fish and other ingredients,** like cucumber and avocado. The fish should be in a container in a cool area, refrigerated, or on ice.

- **Clean, damp towel** to wipe off rice and to moisten the cutting board. This prevents rice from sticking to the board.

- **Wasabi** placed in a small ramekin for making nigiri.

Uramaki

Begin by placing a half sheet of nori on your cutting board, rough side up. Lightly wet your hands with cold water. Grab a handful of rice, about 3 ounces (85g), and shape into an oval. Push the rice firmly over the top-left corner of the nori, making sure to leave a ¼-inch (6mm) gap at the top. Spread the rice from left to right, pressing the rice firmly onto the nori. Create an even 1 × 1-inch (2.5 × 2.5cm) block of rice across the top. Using eight of your fingers (index to pinky on both hands), spread the rice from top to bottom. Square off any rice that hangs off the nori. Sprinkle a small layer of chives or sesame seeds on the rice. Flip the nori over and, while flipping, wipe the board with a damp towel to remove any loose rice and dampen the board. With the rice side down and the nori facing up, place the fish and other ingredients just above the center. I suggest using two to three ingredients, like salmon, cucumber, and avocado. Avoid stuffing the roll with too many ingredients. Grab the bottom of the nori, wrap all the ingredients, and attach the ends together to close the roll. Use the plastic-wrapped makisu to firmly press the roll. I like to create a bit of a tunnel shape for my rolls. Flip the roll forward, and firmly press to ensure it's sealed. Roll it back upright and press again. Slice the roll in half, and bring the two halves side by side. Cut in half again and repeat the process to create a total of eight pieces.

Nigiri

Start by slicing the fish into nigiri pieces. To do so, place the cleaned, gutted, and scaled fish 3 inches (7.5cm) from the close edge of the cutting board, which should be flush with the counter. Using a yanagiba or another sharp, long knife, slice the fish with a single stroke starting from the heel of the knife and finishing with the tip of the knife. Using the entire length of the blade puts the least amount of downward pressure on the fish, resulting in the cleanest cut of nigiri. The trick is to slice the pieces the same length and width, about 4 inches (10cm) long, 2 inches (5cm) wide, and ¼ inch (6mm) thick. Adjust the angle of the knife slightly with each piece to account for the change in size of the fish as you cut.

Now that you have the fish sliced, it's time to make nigiri. In your nondominant hand, lay a slice of fish across your four fingers just above the palm. With your dominant hand, grab a small ball of sushi rice, about ⅓ ounce (10g). While holding the rice, use the index finger of your dominant hand to scoop a small dab of wasabi, and add it to the center of the fish. Place the ball of sushi rice on top of the wasabi, and lightly press the rice into the fish. Rotate the fish so the rice is touching your fingers and the fish is on top. Use the middle finger and thumb of your dominant hand to press the sides of the nigiri together. Then use your index finger to press the top of the fish into the rice. Rotate the nigiri 180 degrees, and repeat the last two steps. It takes patience and practice to get it perfect.

Temaki (Hand Rolls)

Start with a half sheet of nori in your nondominant hand. Place the left side of the nori in your palm. Grab a small handful of rice with your right hand, about 1½ ounces (43g). Place the rice down so it covers the top-left quarter of the nori sheet (for right-handed people; for left-handed folks, place the rice so it covers the top-right quarter of the nori). Place the desired ingredients over the rice. Starting with the bottom corner of the nori that is closest to your palm (bottom left for right-handed people, bottom right for left-handed), roll the nori upward.

Another method is to cut 2 inches (5cm) off the length of the nori. Stick a single grain of rice to the bottom-left corner of the larger piece of nori (again, for right-handed folks; bottom-right corner for left-handed), and attach the cut piece of nori so it extends down like a flap. Follow the method above, but use the flap to cover the ingredients before rolling the nori into a cylindrical shape.

The key to making good hand rolls is to keep the nori dry and crispy. Avoid touching anything with any moisture. Keep your nondominant hand (your "nori hand") completely dry. Eat the hand roll immediately after making it, and never let it sit around. Sushi chefs working at the sushi counter always serve customers their hand rolls directly and tell them to eat them right away so as not to miss the perfect moment.

Chirashi

First, slice the ingredients into bite-size pieces. You can use sashimi pieces or smaller. Place the sushi rice in a bowl, and top with your desired ingredients. Drizzle with soy sauce, and enjoy with a side of wasabi. The great thing is you can use a large variety of raw fish or no fish at all.

Scan for bonus content.

Hosomaki

Start with a half sheet of nori, rough side up. Take a small handful of sushi rice, about 2 ounces (55g). Place the rice onto the nori and spread it from left to right, making sure to leave a ¼-inch (6mm) gap at the top of the seaweed. Spread a thin layer of rice across the entire sheet of nori, keeping that ¼-inch (6mm) gap on top. Place the nori onto a makisu with the bottom of the nori aligned with the bottom of the makisu. Place one to two ingredients along the length of the nori. Grab the bottom of the nori and makisu at the same time and fold over the ingredients, rolling the nori toward the top. Lift the makisu, and roll it over to seal the nori together. Press firmly two to three times, and release it onto the cutting board. Cut the roll in half, line up the two halves side by side, and cut into thirds to create six pieces.

Sashimi

Before slicing sashimi pieces, most fish are salt-cured for a short period.

Start by wiping a baking sheet with a slightly damp towel. Sprinkle salt evenly and generously across the tray. Place the fish filet skin-side down and then sprinkle another light layer of salt on the flesh. Let it sit in the refrigerator for 20 minutes. You will notice some moisture that has been pulled out by the salt. Rinse the filet under cold water, and pat dry with paper towels.

Slice the fish into a saku—a uniform boneless block of fish ready for sashimi. Sashimi is usually skinless, but some preparations allow for the skin to be included. In this book, I include a recipe for snapper sashimi with its skin on (see page 116).

Tender fish like tuna, salmon, and yellowtail can be sliced relatively thick at ¼ inch (6mm) or ½ inch (1.2cm). Fish with chewier textures like snapper, flounder, grouper, and other white fish need to be sliced thinner than ¼ inch (6mm) or as thin as possible.

Slicing fish is simple if you use a sharp knife. Opt for a yanagiba or the sharpest knife you have to make long, single strokes. Start with the heel of the knife on the fish, and slice all the way through, finishing at the tip of the knife.

If the saku is at least 1 inch (2.5cm) tall, cut straight down. If it's less than 1 inch (2.5cm) tall, slice at an angle so that once the sashimi is cut, the width of the saku is 1 inch (2.5cm). The shorter the saku, the steeper the angle the knife needs to be.

Traditionally, plating starts with thin slices of daikon radish and a shiso leaf, aka a perilla leaf. Then a few pieces of sashimi are placed in front of the shiso leaf. Serve with wasabi and soy sauce.

Safely Enjoying Raw Wild Fish

The question I get asked most is, "Is it safe to eat fish raw?" The answer is a nuanced yes and no. When eating raw fish, I follow this simple rule of thumb: never eat freshwater fish raw. Fresh water carries a lot of bacteria. Whether you freeze it or not, bacteria still exist on and in the fish. Would you drink fresh water out of a stream, river, or lake without boiling it? Probably not. (At least, you shouldn't, because of the bacteria in the water. Boiling the water kills the bacteria.) I follow the same rule for freshwater fish: cook it. Here are some other questions I'm frequently asked about eating raw fish.

When is saltwater fish safe to eat raw?

Many saltwater fish can be eaten raw straight out of the ocean. How is this possible? The bacteria that exist in fresh water do not survive in salt water. Assuming there is no cross contamination, saltwater fish are safe for immediate raw consumption. However, there is still a possibility of parasites being present.

Is it safe to eat saltwater fish with parasitic worms in them?

Yes, you can make saltwater fish with worms or parasites in them completely safe to eat. One way to ensure the worms are dead is simply by cooking the fish to an internal temperature of 145°F (63°C).

What if I want to eat the fish raw?

Many types of parasites exist in ocean fish, but in this case, we are talking about parasitic worms. The two types of parasitic fish worms are roundworms (nematodes) and tapeworms (cestodes). If eaten in their live state, they may cause some health concerns but most likely not death. To consume the fish safely, the Food and Drug Administration (FDA) recommends freezing it to -31°F (-35°C) for 15 hours or to -4°F (-20°C) for 7 days. The most crucial thing here is to ensure the filet is fully frozen. To test that, take two pieces of frozen fish and tap them together. They should make a high-pitched noise, almost as if you're tapping metal on metal. At this point, the worms are dead, and the fish is safe for raw preparations. Defrost the fish by transferring it to the fridge for 24 hours or by leaving it in a cold-water bath for 1 to 3 hours depending on the size. Do not place the fish filets directly in water; instead, make sure they are sealed in a plastic bag. Eating raw fish has potential dangers, so consume at your own risk.

What if I accidentally eat a live parasite?

Most often, swallowing a live nematode is harmless. It will pass straight through your intestines without any issue. In rare cases, swallowing a nematode larva can cause a severe upset stomach if it attaches to the intestinal lining, an infection called anisakiasis. Humans are not suitable hosts for nematodes, so they will live a maximum of seven to ten days in the human digestive tract.

What types of fish are least likely to have parasitic worms?

Pelagic species are less likely to have parasitic worms and include tuna (bluefin, bigeye, skipjack, bonito, albacore), wahoo, Spanish mackerel, and mahi mahi. These are good species to eat raw, straight out of the ocean. Fish like snapper, hogfish, trevally or jacks, triggerfish, sea robins or gurnards, John Dory, seabass, barracuda, kahawai, cod, and mackerel can all have parasites, and they should either be frozen or eaten raw with precaution.

What types of fish are most likely to have parasitic worms?

Salmon, halibut, and yellowtail, which are all popular fish used for sushi, can contain parasitic worms. Wild salmon should always be frozen before consuming raw. You may have seen some footage online of Alaskan bears walking around with long tapeworms sticking out of their butts. That's because they eat raw salmon without freezing it first (obviously). The worms do no harm to the bear, but it's still gross. Yellowtail can have parasites as well.

What about salmon that lives in fresh water and salt water (aka anadromous fish)?

Salmon spend only their first year in fresh water. By the time they're caught, they have likely been in salt water for two to four years. So, I treat salmon as saltwater fish. Any bacteria from fresh water would not continue to exist after living in salt water for that long. Some people say to freeze salmon because they've lived in fresh water, and therefore, you need to kill the bacteria. Well, freezing does not kill bacteria, but cooking does. The reason salmon is frozen is to kill parasites. Salmon often carry tapeworms, which is a parasite they get from their freshwater juvenile stage. Tapeworms can be killed with proper freezing.

What about landlocked freshwater salmon?

These salmon spend their entire lives in fresh water. Therefore, I would follow the first rule of thumb: Don't eat freshwater fish raw.

How do I check for parasites?

If you want to eat your fish raw, straight out of the ocean, there are a couple of safety measures you can take. These methods are not 100 percent foolproof, especially if you lack experience with fresh fish.

For most fish, it's common to find parasites on the belly filets closest to the anal fin. For this reason, when I have a halibut over 30 inches (76cm) long, I often save the belly loin for cooking and use the shoulder loin for raw preparations.

Another safety check is the candling method. After the fish is fileted and skinned, hold the entire filet up to a bright light. The filet will be translucent enough that you might be able to spot a few parasites. People often mix up bacteria and parasites—bacteria are not visible to the naked eye, but parasites are. They might be super small, so it's possible to miss them, but in general, parasites will be visible. With some white fish, like snapper, you'll see small, squiggly lines in the filets, but those are just blood vessels.

Should I throw the fish away if I find parasites?

No! You can simply remove the section that has the parasites. The rest of the meat will still be safe to eat raw. If you're uncomfortable with this method, save the rest of the fish to cook. I recently saw a video that had gone viral because someone found a live worm in a piece of salmon from Costco. I looked at the label and saw that it said "fresh wild Alaskan sockeye," which explains why there was a worm in it. This is natural! So at least you know the label is accurate. I would 100 percent eat that fish over a farm-raised salmon any day.

Lastly, if you're still unsure, just cook it. That is the guaranteed safe method, even if the fish has parasites.

Why do you prefer wild fish to farmed fish?

There is a lot of controversy around farmed fish, in particular farmed salmon. The controversies mainly come from what it takes to feed the farms and the potential diseases it might transfer to the wild fish population. Most of the salmon found in supermarkets and even sushi restaurants in the US is farmed Atlantic salmon. When it comes to sustainability of seafood, we always say choose local. One advantage of farmed fish is that they are less likely to have worms because fish farms are able to control the feed of the fish.

Eating Raw Shellfish

Shellfish is categorized into two types: crustaceans (crabs, lobsters, etc.) and mollusks (octopuses, clams, oysters, etc.) Shellfish are mostly safe to consume raw, but do not eat raw freshwater shellfish such as freshwater clams and prawns. While doing research on parasitic worms, I learned that it's possible for octopuses, squid, and shrimp to have worms, and though I've eaten these species raw and have never encountered worms in them, the literature says it's still a possibility, so caution is advised.

The most common shellfish to eat raw are oysters, but you can also eat raw clams and cockles, mussels, shrimp, squid, and octopuses! Let's talk about each one, and I'll explain why they're better enjoyed raw.

- **Clams** in my opinion have the most flavor pound for pound. They are one of the most delicious and easy-to-acquire species of seafood. Raw clams are better than raw oysters as they are a little less briny, sweeter, and saltier. If you love oysters straight out of the shell, give clams a try. When it comes to shellfish, fresher is always better. Popular types eaten raw are cherrystone clams, surf clams, and chocolate clams (Mexico). Some of my favorites that I've harvested myself include horseneck clams, butter clams, New Zealand pipis, razor clams, manila clams, and littleneck clams. So, I guess, all of them! They really are so good. For more about harvesting clams, see page 148.

- **Mussels** are one of those shellfish species that not many people are into. I'll admit, I don't really care for them either. That is, until I taste one. Every time I have one, without a doubt I ask myself, "Why don't I eat this more often?" The thing with mussels is that the meat itself is good, but the juices are the real star. Sauces and soups made with mussels are heavily packed with delicious ocean flavor. For example, cioppino wouldn't be the same without it. What about raw mussels? I've tried it once or twice, but I don't personally care for it. It felt slippery and tasted bitter, but some people swear by them, so I might have to give it another try soon.

- **Scallops** are soft, tender, and sweet. There's no doubt that they're great in any style of preparation, but they're best raw. When talking about scallops, we're actually referring to the adductor muscle of the bivalve. Clams, mussels, and oysters also have adductors, but scallops' are the biggest.

- **Shrimp or prawns,** specifically spot prawns, aka amaebi or botan ebi, might be the sweetest and creamiest of all the seafood species when prepared raw. (*Amaebi* literally translates to "sweet shrimp" in Japanese.) They are commonly found in sushi restaurants across the US. You can also catch them yourself in the US. For more on shrimp, see page 153.

- **Squid** is a favorite of all! From fish to crab to people, everything and everybody love squid. The flavor and sustainability of the species is unmatched. Squid have a six-to-ten-month lifespan, which is extremely short, meaning there's typically no accumulation of toxins in their systems and that they have a rapid growth and reproduction rate. Raw squid preparations can be mildly sweet and creamy. If they're extremely fresh, they're a little bit crunchy. As I mentioned earlier, squid and octopuses can carry roundworms, but I've never personally seen any in either. If you feel safer freezing them before consuming raw, feel free to do so. I've eaten many of them straight out of the water.

- **Octopuses** are underrated when it comes to raw preparations. Not many places prepare raw octopus, but some Japanese restaurants serve a dish called tako wasabi, which mixes raw octopus tentacles and wasabi. Octopuses have an extremely chewy texture, which is pleasant in the same way we enjoy chewing gum. I can't figure out any other way to explain "chewy" as being enjoyable for the Western palate. In Asian cuisine, especially Japanese and Korean, we enjoy different textures in our food that are not as popular in the West. In Japanese foods, there are many more ways of explaining and expressing textures than just describing flavor. I think that shows the importance of texture in our cuisine.

- **Uni** is creamy and sweet and becomes bitter and sour as it ages. Depending on the source, they all have a slightly unique flavor. My favorite variety is the purple urchin found abundantly along the coast of California.

Toxins in Fish and Shellfish

Paralytic Shellfish Poisoning

The biggest concern for wild-harvested shellfish is the algae bloom in bivalves, such as clams, oysters, scallops, and mussels. An algae bloom, often referred to as the red tide, is an exponential growth of phytoplankton that can produce toxins. Bivalves feed by filtering water through their system, meaning the toxins can build up in their tissue. The toxin, which cooking does not destroy, can cause paralytic shellfish poisoning, which can lead to severe illness and even death. Luckily, once the algae bloom is over, bivalves filter clean sea water and will once again be safe for consumption within a couple of weeks.

Algae blooms can happen any time of the year but are most likely to happen in the summer. You may have heard the phrase, "Eat shellfish only in months with the letter r," (September to April). This is a good general rule of thumb. However, in California, it's still warm in September and October, so the California Department of Public Health recommends not consuming wild bivalves until November, which adjusts the season for shellfish fishing in California from November to April. During this time, the water is tested on a regular basis. There is a toll-free number you can call to check for recent updates and the safe consumption of wild shellfish: (800) 553-4133. Search local regulations and guidelines on wild shellfish consumption wherever you plan to fish.

The effects of shellfish poisoning set in within 15 minutes and include a tingling sensation of the lips and tongue. In a survival situation, you can touch your lips to the meat of the clams or oysters to check for the toxin. Do not try this for regular consumption.

As filter feeders, shellfish literally are what they eat. If a toxin is in the water, it's in them too. Polluted water and runoff from recent rain can make shellfish unfit for consumption. All this information might make you never want to eat bivalves ever again, but there are definitely ways to do it safely.

The guts of the shellfish are the parts that are unsafe to consume during the summer months. When eating clams and mussels, you eat the guts and all, but with scallops, people are often still able to eat them during the summer. How? Because you typically eat only the adductor muscle with scallops. If you're like me and like eating all the other parts of the scallop, refrain from doing so in the summer or do so only when clams and mussels are safe for consumption.

Ciguatera

While we're on the topic of toxins, let's talk about ciguatera. Ciguatera is an illness from eating fish that has been contaminated with toxins produced by marine microalgae and is associated with reef fish living in warm, tropical climates. For me, this is scarier than the rest of the toxins, parasites, or bacteria that you might unknowingly ingest in seafood. I've heard many of my friends in the tropics say they or someone they know have gotten this illness. If you spend time in Hawaii, someone will tell you all about it from first- or secondhand experience. Symptoms include nausea, vomiting, weakness, tingling, and neurological problems. The symptoms wouldn't be so bad if they lasted only a day or two, but they can last a month or even longer. There is no official way to tell if a fish has ciguatera, but one method I've heard of from my friend in Samoa is to observe whether or not flies land on the fish—if they don't, the fish has ciguatera. Taste, color, and smell are no different in contaminated fish versus uncontaminated, and cooking does not kill the toxin. The best thing you can do to avoid this illness is simply to avoid eating and catching fish that are likely to be contaminated. Local knowledge will be the most helpful for this. Fish that are likely to have ciguatera are large, predatory reef fish including certain grouper species, moray eels, barracuda, and giant trevally. Larger fish accumulate toxins by eating reef fish and, therefore, have a higher chance of causing ciguatera poisoning. Pelagic fish like tuna, mahi mahi, and wahoo are not exposed to these toxins and are generally safe for consumption.

Fishing

I grew up fishing in Japan with my father. I got my first fishing rod as a Christmas present when I was five years old. We did a bit of bass fishing and some ocean fishing at local piers. When I moved to the US, my uncle John would take me fishing for bass and surf perch. My mom also took us to fish at the piers, where we would usually catch mackerel. I had a long stretch of years during high school and college when I didn't fish, but I got back into it right at the end of college when a friend took me out to catch striped bass in San Francisco Bay. I was hooked once again, and I haven't stopped since.

Most of my fishing experience comes from making YouTube videos with friends in San Francisco Bay, fishing for halibut, lingcod, rockfish, salmon, and Dungeness crabs. I have also fished in Alaska, where I spent two whole summers traveling in our converted Sprinter van. I fish in Japan every time I visit my dad and sister. I've fished in New Zealand, where my partner, Jocelyn, and I spent the greater part of 2023 traveling around in a small, converted van we purchased there. I have experience fishing in the tropical waters of the Pacific, including in Hawaii, Niue, and Samoa. I would love to spend more time fishing in Australia, Central America, and anywhere else that has fish.

The Best Time to Fish

When it comes to fishing, there is so much that goes into the technique: different types of rigs, fishing lines, lures, baits, rods, reels, and methods (like trolling, drifting, etc.). The one tip I can give you that seems to be true for most inshore fishing is to fish the tides. Pay attention to whether it's peak high tide or peak low tide as fish tend to be more active and feed two hours before and after a peak tide. Tides are always predictable and are the one thing you can count on always being true.

The weather varies so much, but it should always be taken into account before you head out to fish. Wind is a big factor that affects castability, the boat's drift, and even safety. Whenever I fish, I'm looking for winds less than 20 miles per hour (32kmph). Another factor with ocean fishing is the swell. Whether on a boat or fishing from shore, swells can make or break your day. Wherever I'm fishing, I'm looking for swells less than 6 feet (1.8m) high. If you consider these two weather patterns along with the tide, you will raise your success rate of catching fish.

Coastal Foraging

I began coastal foraging in college when I realized there was so much available right in our backyard. I picked up a book called *The Sea Forager's Guide to the Northern California Coast* by Kirk Lombard, in which the author goes through nearly every species of fish and shellfish you can harvest in and around the Bay Area. This knowledge is the best resource to start your foraging journey. Foraging requires few tools and is a much cheaper investment than fishing. In most cases, all you'll need are a pair of boots, a bucket, a pocketknife, and gloves.

The best time to go coastal foraging is during low tides. In California, the tide varies anywhere from 6.8 feet (2m) at the highest to -1.8 feet (-0.5m) at the lowest (aka king tide). King tide is the best time to go foraging, but as it occurs only twice a year, any negative tide is a great time to get out and forage.

On the West Coast of the US, you can expect to find a variety of seaweed and kelp, crabs (brown, red rock, and Dungeness), mussels, clams (littleneck, manila, butter or Washington, razor, horseneck, and geoduck), sea urchins (purple and red), and octopuses (two-spot, common octopus, and giant Pacific), all while coastal foraging in the tidepools. A fishing license is required to take any of these species in all West Coast states, so check local regulations. For example, in California, you must harvest an octopus by hand or by hook and line; any other method is considered illegal. There may be specific species that are off-limits in certain areas, particularly Marine Protected Areas (MPAs), where the catching of all marine creatures is illegal. There may also be size restrictions for various species, which vary by state. You can find all this information by looking up fishing regulations through the Department of Fish and Wildlife.

Japanese and Asian Ingredients

To start cooking Japanese and other Asian cuisines, you'll need to know these basic ingredients and what they're used for. I cover several basic ingredients and recipes in this book, but there are many more you can uncover yourself. Throughout this book, I've tried to use ingredients that can be found in much of the world so that as many people as possible can recreate these recipes. If a specific ingredient is not available to you, experiment with some substitutions. Most of the core ingredients listed here are available at Asian markets around the world or can be found online.

	Description	Use
katsuobushi	Also known as bonito flakes. Made by drying, fermenting, and smoking skipjack tuna to develop a deep umami flavor. Shaved paper thin.	Primarily used for making traditional Japanese dashi (soup stock). It can also be used to garnish food directly, like okonomiyaki or takoyaki, which are famous Japanese street foods.
kombu	Also known as kelp. As sheets of kelp are dried, an amino acid called glutamine rises to the surface, creating the fine, white, powdery crystals on the surface. These fine crystals are the source of the umami flavor used in much of Japanese cooking.	Its main use is for making dashi combined with katsuobushi. The best temperature to extract the flavor out of kombu is in water heated to 140°F (60°C) for 1 hour. Remove kombu when it starts to simmer. Avoid boiling kombu, as it will release slime and bitterness.
wakame	Another type of seaweed. Small individual bits of seaweed dried and sold in bags.	Wakame can be rehydrated and used in miso soup or seaweed salad.

mirin

Sweet rice wine used in Japanese cooking to add sweetness.

Commonly used in Japanese cooking, particularly for sauces, glazes, and marinades, like tare.

sake

Japanese alcohol made from fermented rice.

Often used alongside mirin to add more umami and depth.

dashi

Japanese soup stock that is very savory and filled with umami. Typically homemade by steeping kombu and katsuobushi. Can include dried shiitake mushrooms and dried anchovies for additional flavor.

Used to add umami and complexity in soups like ramen, udon, and miso soup, and also commonly used in sauces to enhance flavor.

hondashi

Flavorful powder that makes instant dashi broth when added to hot water. Hondashi translates to "real broth."

Used as a shortcut for homemade dashi. Broth made from hondashi can be used whenever dashi is called for in a recipe.

usukuchi shoyu

Light-flavored soy sauce. This soy sauce has a shorter fermentation time than regular soy sauce, which gives it a lighter color, a slight sweetness, and less saltiness.

This can be used in any dish for which you would use soy sauce. It's great for dishes like ikura, when you want to add soy sauce flavor without the dark color. It's also great in stir-fries to add a light saltiness.

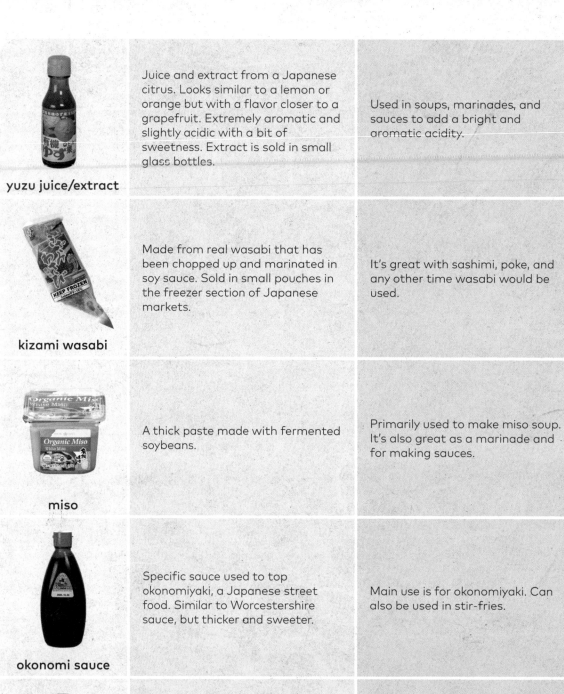

yuzu juice/extract

Juice and extract from a Japanese citrus. Looks similar to a lemon or orange but with a flavor closer to a grapefruit. Extremely aromatic and slightly acidic with a bit of sweetness. Extract is sold in small glass bottles.

Used in soups, marinades, and sauces to add a bright and aromatic acidity.

kizami wasabi

Made from real wasabi that has been chopped up and marinated in soy sauce. Sold in small pouches in the freezer section of Japanese markets.

It's great with sashimi, poke, and any other time wasabi would be used.

miso

A thick paste made with fermented soybeans.

Primarily used to make miso soup. It's also great as a marinade and for making sauces.

okonomi sauce

Specific sauce used to top okonomiyaki, a Japanese street food. Similar to Worcestershire sauce, but thicker and sweeter.

Main use is for okonomiyaki. Can also be used in stir-fries.

Kewpie mayo

Umami-rich and tangy Japanese mayo.

This can be used anywhere regular mayo is applicable. It's used often to top okonomiyaki and takoyaki and is great in sandwiches and coleslaw.

furikake

Dry rice seasoning that often includes small bits of nori, sesame seeds, and dried fish.

Its main use is to sprinkle over steamed rice. It's used often for poke.

sushinoko

Sushi rice vinegar in powder form.

This powder can be added directly to cooked white rice to make sushi rice. It's the easiest method for making sushi rice.

gochugaru

Korean red chili peppers dried in the sun and pulverized into a coarse powder. Mildly spicy and slightly sweet.

This is great to add to soups and sauces.

gochujang

Fermented Korean red chili paste that's savory, sweet, and spicy.

This is used to make soups, marinades, and sauces and is commonly used to make kimchi paste.

fish sauce

Salty, flavorful sauce made from fish or krill that has been salted and fermented for two years. A staple ingredient in Southeast Asian cuisine.

Its main use is to make sauces and dips. It can also be added to any cooking to enhance the salt level.

BASICS

Rice Without Measurements

yield **1 cup uncooked rice feeds 2–4 people** | prep **3 minutes** | cook **30 minutes**

It's important to know how to make rice without measuring. Rather than giving you actual measurements, this recipe explains how to cook rice, which will ultimately help you become a more intuitive cook. No matter how much rice you want to make, this method will work.

1 In a medium bowl, wash the rice under cold water by filling the bowl, gently stirring the rice, and then draining the cloudy water. Repeat 3 to 5 times until the water runs clear.

2 Transfer the washed rice to a pot and level the rice so it sits perfectly flat. Use your index finger as a guideline and place it so your fingertip touches the top of the rice. Then, add water to the pot until it reaches just under your first knuckle.

3 Place the pot over high heat. Start a timer for 20 minutes.

4 When the water comes to a boil, cover with a lid and reduce the heat to low. Keep on low until the timer expires.

5 Take the pot off the heat and let it rest for 10 minutes, covered, to finish the cooking process.

Medium- or short-grain white rice

Note
This method will not work at higher elevations. For every 5,000 feet (1.5km) of elevation, add 25 percent more cook time and water. This method also may not work if you're cooking outdoors when it's either windy or cold. It becomes a bit tricky under these conditions, but it can be done. Keep the rice at a boil for about 15 minutes, then reduce to medium heat for 5 minutes before removing from the heat. Just before turning off the heat, increase the heat to high for 10 seconds. Then, look at how much water is left. If you see any liquid bubbling, it needs additional time. If there's only steam, the rice is done.

Master Sushi Rice

serves **4** | prep **20 minutes** | cook **30 minutes**

Sushi rice is one of the more difficult things to get right. It requires a lot of technique and traditionally requires the use of a hangiri, a flat wooden bowl used for sushi preparation. The large, flat surface area allows the rice to cool quickly. If you're preparing for more than four people, multiply the recipe to create the desired amount. Japanese rice is best for sushi, but be sure to use either short- or medium-grain rice. I often use koshihikari, which is widely available at Asian markets. I also recommend using a heavy-bottomed pot; stainless steel is a good option, but Dutch ovens work well too.

1   In a small bowl or pitcher, combine 1½ cups (375ml) cold water and the kombu. Set aside.

2   In a separate bowl, wash the rice with cold water quickly but gently, being careful not to break the grains of rice. Strain into a sieve. Repeat 3 to 5 times until the water runs clear.

3   To eliminate broken grains, place the strained rice into a medium bowl and add water until the empty and broken grains float to the top. Carefully pour the water out, stopping before any rice pours out. Repeat 3 to 5 times, then strain. Allow the rice to dry in the strainer for 10 minutes.

4   Transfer the rice to a large, heavy-bottomed pot. Strain the kombu from the water and add the water to the rice. Let soak for 10 minutes.

5   Cover and heat, first on high for about 10 minutes or until the water starts to boil, then immediately reduce to low, for a total of 20 minutes.

6   Increase the heat to high for 10 seconds, remove the pot from the stove, and let rest for 10 minutes with the lid on.

7   Transfer the hot rice to a wide, shallow bowl or hangiri. Immediately add the vinegar, spreading it around to saturate every grain of rice.

8   Using a rice paddle in a cutting motion, stir the rice to allow each grain to mix with the vinegar. Do not overmix as it will cause the rice to become mushy.

9   Let the rice cool for 10 minutes. If you're in a warm environment, use a fan to cool the rice as quickly as possible before moving on to creating your sushi.

3 x 3-in (8 x 8cm) piece of kombu
2 cups (400g) short-grain rice
½ cup (125ml) sushi vinegar

Note
The rice needs to be hot when you add the vinegar so it can absorb it all. Then, it needs to be cooled down quickly. Sushi rice will last 36 hours without refrigeration due to the high vinegar content.

Scan for bonus content.

Sushi Vinegar

makes **about 4¼ cups (1L)** | prep **5 minutes** | cook **1 minute**

Outside of Japan, people often refer to raw fish as sushi, but what people do not realize is that the key to sushi is vinegared rice. The first part of the word, *su*, means "vinegar," and the second part, *shi*, means "rice." Therefore, *sushi* translates to "vinegared rice." It is often combined with raw fish, but this is not always the case. If you buy rice labeled "sushi rice," it refers to rice used to make sushi but without the vinegar included. You need to add the vinegar—mixed with salt, sugar, and kombu—yourself to make sushi rice. Note: It's a lot more sugar than you might expect.

3⅓ cups (825ml) rice vinegar
1⅔ cups (300g) brown sugar
½ cup (150g) salt
⅓ cup (14g) kombu (dried kelp)

1 In a medium saucepan, combine the rice vinegar, brown sugar, and salt. Place over medium-high heat, and stir until the sugar and salt have dissolved.

2 Turn off the heat and add the kombu. Let it cool, and use right away or keep stored in a container with the kombu.

Note
If you want to make a smaller or larger amount, you can take the same ratio of ingredients and make as little or as much as you like. The finished product with its strong vinegar base will keep for months without refrigeration.

Scan for bonus content.

Tare

makes **2½ cups (625ml)** | prep **1 minute** | cook **20 minutes**

Tare means "sauce" in Japanese. This can be a base for ramen, a sauce to glaze yakitori, or a marinade for fish or chicken. Each can vary in ingredients and cook time, but here is a basic tare recipe to get things started. You can add ingredients like bonito flakes, kombu, dried fish, or mushrooms to introduce deeper flavors.

1⅔ cups (400ml) soy sauce
½ cup (125ml) mirin
½ cup (125ml) sake
¼ cup (50g) brown sugar

1 In a medium saucepan, combine all the ingredients and bring to a simmer while stirring. Simmer for 20 minutes.

2 Allow the sauce to cool to room temperature. Transfer to a jar and store in the refrigerator for up to 6 months.

Note
For ramen bases, add 1 part tare to 10 parts stock (fish, chicken, beef, or vegetable).

Dashi (Japanese Stock)

makes **about 6⅓ cups (1.5L)** | prep **1 minute** | cook **5 minutes**

Dashi is essential for Japanese cooking, as it's the base of most soups and sauces. Miso soup, udon, ramen, and chawanmushi are just a few dishes that use dashi as a base. While hondashi can be used as a quick shortcut for homemade dashi (much like using chicken bouillon instead of making chicken stock), homemade dashi has more nuanced flavor and can be customized to your taste. There are additional ingredients you can use to make dashi, but this is the most basic recipe.

1 To a medium pot, add 6⅓ cups (1.5L) cold water and the kombu. Slowly bring to a boil over medium-low heat.

2 Just before the water comes to a boil, remove the kombu.

3 When the water begins to boil, turn off the heat and add the katsuobushi. Let steep for 5 minutes, then strain through a fine-mesh sieve. Add the salt.

½ cup (14g) kombu
1 cup (12g) katsuobushi
   (bonito flakes)
½ tsp (3g) salt

Note
The best way to extract flavor from kombu is by using cold water, not boiling water. If you have the time, combine the cold water and kombu 4 hours before boiling or even the night before. The kombu and katsuobushi can be used afterward to make a rice topping by chopping it and mixing in soy sauce to taste.

Ponzu

makes **1¾ cups (425ml)** | prep **2 minutes** | cook **None**

Ponzu is an acidic, citrus-flavored soy sauce. It's light and flavorful, pairing well with raw fish and salads. You can buy it premade, but if you ever need to make some at home, it's really easy.

In a small bowl or jar, combine all of the ingredients, making sure to strain out any citrus seeds from the juice. Store in the refrigerator for up to 2 months.

½ cup (125ml) soy sauce
1 cup (250ml) dashi or water
¼ cup (60ml) freshly squeezed citrus juice of your choice (lemon, lime, orange, grapefruit, or a mix)

Note
If you need a smaller amount, simply keep the same ratio:
2 parts soy sauce,
4 parts dashi or water,
1 part citrus juice.

Umami Soy Sauce

makes **about 1⅔ cups (400ml)** | prep **1 minute, plus overnight to soak** | cook **None**

Katsuobushi and kombu infuse soy sauce with umami, and the resulting extra-flavorful soy sauce can be used in several different ways. Use it as regular soy sauce for sashimi or dilute it to make shoyu-dashi (10 parts water to 1 part umami soy sauce) or ramen base (10 parts pork broth to 1 part umami soy sauce). It's nice to have a jar of this handy in the fridge to make any of these or even to add to stir-fries and fried rice.

12oz (355ml) light soy sauce
1 cup (12g) katsuobushi (bonito flakes)
¼ cup (7g) kombu

1 In a small bowl, combine all of the ingredients. Let soak overnight.

2 Strain the liquid into a jar (discard the solids). Store in the refrigerator for up to 2 months.

Note
Keep the same ratio of ingredients to make more or less umami soy sauce, as desired.

Thai Chili Fish Sauce

makes **about ½ cup (125ml)** | prep **2 minutes** | cook **None**

Thai chili fish sauce is a must-have in the fridge at all times. This sauce is traditionally made in a mortar and pestle to bring out all the flavors from the chili and garlic, but it can also be made by simply chopping everything and combining. The fish sauce brings richness and umami, and the Thai chilis add flavorful and intense heat. It's a great sauce to go on so many different dishes, especially fish and rice. My favorite way to use this sauce is for breakfast over rice and a fried egg. It's also great on noodles—add some of this to peanut sauce and crushed peanuts, and mix it all together.

2 tbsp (18g) chopped fresh Thai chilis
4 garlic cloves, chopped
½ cup (30g) chopped cilantro
1 tbsp (12g) sugar
5 tbsp (75ml) fish sauce
2 tbsp (30ml) lime juice

If using a mortar and pestle, add the Thai chilis, garlic, cilantro, and sugar to the mortar. Using the pestle, crush and grind the ingredients together. Add the fish sauce and lime juice, and mix well with a spoon. (Alternatively, you can combine all the ingredients in a small bowl, and mix until the sugar is completely dissolved.)

Vietnamese Dipping Sauce

makes **about 1 cup (250ml)** | prep **5 minutes** | cook **None**

Someone once told me the trick to making this sauce is by first making a good lemonade and then adding fish sauce, garlic, and chili. I'm not sure where this method came from or if it's legit, but it works! Combine this sauce with rice noodles and a protein for a great meal any time of the day.

½ cup (125ml) lemon juice
1 tbsp (12g) cane sugar
2 tbsp (30ml) fish sauce
1 tsp (3g) fresh or dry chili flakes
4 garlic cloves, chopped

1   In a small bowl, combine the lemon juice, sugar, and ¼ cup (60ml) water. Mix thoroughly until the sugar is dissolved.

2   Add the fish sauce, chili, and garlic, and mix well to combine.

Pickle Brine for Pickling

makes **2 cups (450g)** | prep **4 minutes** | cook **2 minutes**

There are a few different components in a dish that enhance flavor. Salt is the most obvious one. Another is acid, like lemon juice or vinegar. One you may not know about is pickle brine. Pickles not only add a textural component with a crunch but also enhance the flavor of the dish. This pickle brine recipe is my go-to, and it works to pickle anything from onions to kelp, or even fish. The habanero peppers are hot and add a floral flavor that goes well with the acidic vinegar.

⅔ cup (150ml) rice vinegar
2 tsp (12g) salt
1 tsp (4g) cane sugar
1 habanero pepper, sliced
4 garlic cloves, sliced
6 peppercorns, lightly crushed
Pickling ingredient of your choice

1 In a small pot, combine the rice vinegar, ⅔ cup (150ml) water, salt, and sugar. Bring to a low simmer over medium heat.

2 To a quart-size mason jar, add the habanero, garlic, peppercorns, and the pickling ingredient of your choice (enough to fill the jar). Pour the hot vinegar mixture into the jar, being sure to cover the ingredients completely. Place the lid on, allow it to cool on the counter, and then store in the refrigerator.

Pickled Red Onion

makes **2 cups (450g)** | prep **5 minutes** | cook **1 minute, plus 30 minutes to cool**

This spicy pickled red onion is so good in just about any dish. It's super easy to make and lasts a very long time in the fridge. It gives a nice crunch and spice, but most importantly adds acidity. This can be added to burgers, hot dogs, fish tacos, fried fish, barbecued meat, and even raw clams.

½ cup (120ml) rice vinegar
1 tbsp (18g) salt
¼ tbsp (3g) white sugar
1 red onion, sliced
2 garlic cloves, sliced
1 habanero pepper, sliced
8 black peppercorns

1 In a medium pot, combine the rice vinegar, salt, sugar, and ½ cup (125ml) water. Heat over medium heat until the salt and sugar have dissolved, just before the mixture simmers. Remove from the heat.

2 In a quart-size mason jar or similar container, combine the red onion, garlic, habanero, and peppercorns. Pour the hot vinegar mixture over the top, making sure everything is covered. Seal the jar and allow it to cool. Store in the refrigerator.

FISH

Salmon

The Tongass National Forest, the largest intact temperate rainforest of the world, comprises a large portion of the Pacific Northwest where salmon is a keystone species. They are deeply rooted to the animals, land, and people of the region. Salmon provides an important food source for animals like orcas, birds, bears, and more. As the spawning season approaches, each salmon returns to their birth river after being out at sea for two to five years. During their return, they're picked off by bears that are in much need of a reliable and fatty food source. When bears walk off into the woods with their catch, the head and carcass remain in the forest, fertilizing and providing nutrients for the land, trees, and plants. Old growth trees of the Tongass absorb much of the carbon in the atmosphere, fighting ocean acidification, which in turn provides a healthy ecosystem for the fish to spawn and thrive. The native peoples of the region, such as the Tlingit, Tsimshian, and Haida, have been stewards of the land and sea for millennia. Their cultures are intertwined with the life cycles of salmon, providing not only sustenance but also art, tradition, and cultural heritage. To learn more, check out the Sitka Conservation Society and my short film on YouTube, *Tongass National Forest.*

Scan for bonus content.

For a long time, I didn't like the flavor of salmon. That all changed when I started catching my own salmon and realized it was just farmed salmon I wasn't into. On the West Coast of the US, we have five different species of wild salmon: pink salmon, aka humpy; chum or dog salmon, aka keta; coho salmon, aka silver; sockeye salmon, aka red; and chinook salmon, aka king. They all have unique characteristics in terms of texture and flavor, but all are better than farmed Atlantic salmon. Parasites in wild salmon are completely normal and perfectly safe to eat as long as the salmon is cooked properly or frozen to kill the parasites (see page 34).

The king salmon is held in high regard for most people. Its rich, fatty, oily, and tender, flaky meat separates itself from the rest of the pack. Sockeye salmon, on the other hand, is very lean and firm, but its red-colored flesh gives it the visually attractive advantage, making it highly sought after among chefs. Coho sits in between the two, as it's not too fatty and not too lean, giving it a great balance of flavor and texture. The next two species, pink and chum salmon, are oftentimes overlooked by most people. The pink salmon is soft, delicate, and sometimes mushy, which gives it a disadvantage, but smoking it or cooking it with a nice sear will yield a delicious fish. The chum salmon is the most underrated of the salmon species. Its texture is not as firm as sockeye, but it is very lean, firm, and mild-flavored. Not only are the filets good, but chum salmon also have the biggest roe of any salmon, and I hold that to a high regard.

The best place to catch salmon is in Alaska. Having spent multiple summers traveling freely and driving our converted Sprinter van throughout Alaska, I can say with confidence that there is no place like it. The scenery is breathtaking, and the fishing is bonkers. By bonkers, I mean you'll literally be busy bonking fish the entire time. It has to be one of the greatest fisheries in the world. The entire summer is salmon season, and the coolest thing is that each species of salmon takes turns coming into the rivers to spawn, with a lot of overlap between species. In June, the catch is going to be king salmon. By July, the sockeye are coming up the river, followed by pink and chum, lasting all throughout August, with coho right around the corner into September. I have experienced catching all five of these species, but the best fishing I ever had was for coho salmon in September out of Juneau, Alaska. Not only did we catch a ridiculous number of salmon, but we also lost even more. Coho are amazingly acrobatic and often jump out of water while spinning and flipping. Pink salmon are also another fun one to target and are easily fishable from either a kayak or the shore. The most interesting thing about pinks is that they have a strict schedule of

spawning every two years. In Washington state, the fishing community knows that pink salmon spawn on only odd-numbered years. Pink salmon are caught all around the Puget Sound and the surrounding areas.

Even if you cannot make it out to Alaska, many salmon species can be caught along the Pacific Coast from Monterey Bay, California, and north of there. The salmon fishing in California is decent, but you can only catch king salmon (although the state has closed salmon season for two consecutive years as I write this in 2024). The salmon fishing gets better the farther north you go. Oregon has a good fishery out of the Columbia River that is abundant but chaotic at times. Washington has the best salmon fishing out of these three states as they have a run of every kind of salmon, with the exception of pink salmon that returns only in odd-numbered years.

How to Fish for Salmon

Boat: This is the most common way to catch salmon, by trolling or mooching. Trolling is the modern-day method, where the boat is constantly in gear, moving the boat forward at 3 to 5 miles per hour (5–8kmh) with the line in the water behind you. The movement of the boat gives action to the bait. The easiest rig is by tying a 40-pound (18kg) leader with a hoochie on the end and a flasher 3 feet (1m) above, then another 2 to 3 feet (0.6–1m) to a swivel if you're using a down rigger. A mooching rig is a fun way to catch salmon but is more challenging. Rig up the main line to a 3- to 6-ounce (85–170g) banana weight to a 6-foot (1.8m) fluorocarbon leader with two ⅒ size circle hooks baited with herring or anchovy. The boat will drift in the currents while you drop the sinker toward the bottom, wind it up to the surface, and drop it again, repeating until you get a fish. Depending on local regulations, hooks may need to be barbless.

Kayak: I'm a kayak angler, so I always like to brag about how I can catch just about any fish that boats catch but from my kayak. Similar to fishing from a boat, on a kayak, you can either mooch or troll. Most cases, I will troll using a 4- to 6-ounce (113–170g) banana weight with the smallest flasher and a hoochie, which works well with coho salmon. To get the bait to a deeper depth, another option is to use a deep diver instead of a weight. You can also replace the hoochie with a Franco bullet rotator (FBR) or crippled anchovy to run bait. The FBR is my preference, as it assists in spinning the bait really fast as you troll. King salmon especially like the bait when it spins fast.

From shore: You can catch salmon without a boat of any kind during certain times of the year and in certain locations. When I go to Alaska, I always make sure to take pink-colored spinners. My favorite is the flying C. In the Bay Area, salmon come inside the bay in September and are often caught from shore using spinners. Many rivers on the West Coast of the US from the Bay Area to Alaska have salmon running during fall. My preferred method for catching river salmon is the bobber-and-egg setup, with a 40-pound (18kg) braided main line and a sliding bobber to a 6-foot (1.8m), 12-pound (5kg) fluorocarbon leader. On the end, tie an egg loop knot with a size 2 octopus hook. The most effective bait is cured salmon roe. The next best is a soft bead, which mimics a single piece of roe. Again, the use of bait and/or barbed hooks may be prohibited, so be sure to check your local regulations before you go.

What to Look for When Buying Salmon

I love fishing for salmon, and that's what I do myself, but for most people, it might be a stretch. The only other way to get salmon is to buy it. The most common salmon on the market is farmed Atlantic salmon. Farmed salmon is controversial due to concerns about sustainability and environmental factors. The fish are bred to grow fast and crammed into cages, which facilitates the spread of disease. To prevent diseases, the salmon are filled with antibiotics, which can be problematic for the fish and the environment. For these reasons, I recommend purchasing wild-caught salmon whenever possible.

Wild salmon are caught by commercial fishermen using a few different techniques. One is hook-and-line, which is the best sustainable method as it would be impossible to catch every single fish in a school with just a hook and a line. The other methods are gillnetting and seine fishing. Gillnets are set where salmon swim. The mesh allows for their heads to come through but not their bodies, rendering them trapped. Salmon seining uses two boats. The net is anchored on the large boat while a small skiff takes one end of the net, wraps it around schools of fish and closes the loop, trapping fish that are in the circle. These netting methods sound harmful as there can be some bycatch, but the bycatch is generally small because fishermen are able to target specific schools of fish.

Whether you're buying farmed salmon or wild salmon, there are several key factors you can pay attention to. First is a visual check. Look at the eyes, gills, and tail. Are the eyes cloudy or clear? Are the gills bright red or dark? Is the tail dried out, or does it look like it's fresh out of the water? Fresh fish will have clear eyes, bright red gills, and a tail that's not dried out. The smell is a big sign of freshness as well. Fresh fish should not smell very fishy. Next is the touch. If allowed to, push your finger into the body of the fish. Does the meat bounce back or does it stay indented? Is it slimy or dry? The meat should bounce back with little-to-no indentation, and fresh fish have a natural coat of slime that protects them.

When buying salmon filets, there are fewer signs for freshness. The biggest factors are smell and texture. Visually, the redness or the color of the filet doesn't always correlate to freshness. Even wild fish sometimes have pale flesh because the color of the meat depends on the diet of the salmon. The meat side of the fish should not look slimy, as the slime should only be on the skin. The texture should be firm and unbroken, not mushy. The smell should be mild rather than fishy.

Chum Salmon Jerky

makes **12 strips** | prep **10 minutes, plus 1 hour to marinate** | cook **8 hours**

Chum salmon, also known as dog salmon or keta salmon, is very much an underrated and underutilized species of salmon. Many Alaskans consider them to be a lower-grade salmon and use it as food for dogs—hence the name "dog salmon." Alaskans are spoiled when it comes to salmon and eat only the top three species: king, sockeye, and coho. Chum salmon is generally harvested for the roe and then sent to Japan, but there has recently been a rebranding of chum salmon as keta. You can find it in some markets and even Costco.

As a non-Alaskan without preconceived notions of salmon hierarchy, I personally think chum salmon is great. It's lean, and the meat is firm. It's similar to sockeye but not as red, rather a pale orange in color. The lack of fat in chum salmon makes it perfect for jerky, and chum salmon jerky is a great snack while fishing. This preparation requires a dehydrator.

1 To make the marinade, in a small bowl, combine the soy sauce, garlic, wasabi, chives, and 1 cup (250ml) water. Mix well to break up the wasabi paste.

2 Place the salmon in a resealable plastic bag or shallow container, and add the marinade, turning to ensure the fish is fully coated. Refrigerate for 1 to 2 hours.

3 Remove the salmon strips from the marinade and lay flat in a dehydrator, making sure none of the slices overlap. Set the dehydrator to 120°F (50°C) for 8 hours or until fully dried.

4 Allow the salmon jerky to fully cool, then vacuum-seal in bags to store.

2 tbsp (30ml) soy sauce

3 garlic cloves, chopped

1 tbsp (16g) wasabi paste

1 tbsp (3g) finely chopped chives

1lb (450g) chum salmon filet, skinned and sliced into thin strips

Note
Keep refrigerated for 2 to 3 weeks or in the freezer for 4 to 6 months.

Simple Smoked Salmon

serves **4–6** | prep **20 hours** | cook **3 hours**

Smoking is a delicious way to preserve the harvest of a bountiful salmon season. After the fish has been smoked and cooled, it can be vacuum-sealed and stored in the freezer for an easy, anytime snack. A smoker will make your life easier, but it is not necessary. Smoked salmon can also be made on a charcoal grill using hot coals and woodchips.

1 In a large container, such as a food-safe plastic tub or stock pot, combine 1 gallon (3.75L) water, the brown sugar, kosher salt, lemon juice, garlic powder, onion powder, and smoked paprika. Mix thoroughly to make a brine.

2 Cut the salmon into small, square portions, roughly 4 x 4 inches (10 x 10cm). Submerge the salmon in the brine. Cover and refrigerate for 10 to 12 hours.

3 Remove the salmon from the brine and rinse under cold water. Pat dry with a paper towel and rest on a wire rack in a cool room for 6 to 8 hours, after which a pellicle (light crust) will form.

4 Set the smoker to 160°F (70°C) with high smoke. Place the salmon in the smoker skin-side down. Smoke for 3 hours. Once finished, the salmon should have a dark orange color with a dry exterior and golden skin. Immediately remove the salmon from the smoker and let it cool.

5 Enjoy smoked salmon on its own as a snack, or use it in another dish, such as a smoked salmon dip or fried rice.

1 cup (200g) brown sugar
1 cup (200g) kosher salt
½ cup (125ml) freshly squeezed lemon juice
1 tbsp (4g) garlic powder
1 tbsp (4g) onion powder
1 tbsp (4g) smoked paprika
3lb (1.4kg) skin-on salmon filet

Scan for bonus content.

Salmon Scotch Egg

makes **6 Scotch eggs** | prep **20 minutes** | cook **20 minutes**

During a subscriber trip in Alaska, we scored big on sockeye salmon. I hosted a workshop on fileting salmon, and it was many of the subscribers' first times fileting a fish. As expected, there was a lot of meat left on the bones. So I had the group scrape off all the excess meat from the bones, and we made this salmon Scotch egg topped with ikura, aka salmon roe—all while we were camping in beautiful Alaska.

1   Bring a medium pot of water to a boil over high heat. Add 6 eggs and boil for 7 minutes. Transfer the eggs to an ice bath to cool. Once cool, peel the eggs and set aside.

2   Prepare your workstation by putting the panko in one bowl and the cornstarch in a second bowl.

3   In a third bowl, combine the minced salmon, salt, pepper, and smoked paprika. Crack in the remaining egg and mix. If the mixture is wet, add ½ cup (30g) panko and 1 tablespoon (7g) cornstarch into the mix. It should be similar in texture to ground beef when making burger patties.

4   Coat a peeled boiled egg with a generous layer of cornstarch. Using your hands, shape one-sixth of the salmon mixture into a flat patty. Add the egg to the center, and wrap the salmon evenly around the whole egg. Place it in the panko bowl, coat generously, and gently shape it into a ball. Repeat with the rest of the boiled eggs.

5   In a large Dutch oven or cast-iron pan, heat the canola oil over medium heat.

6   When the oil is hot, about 250°F (130°C), gently place three of the balls into the oil. Wait 1 minute before adding the other three balls so as not to drop the temperature of the oil. Remember which ones you added first, and remove them first after frying.

7   If the oil covers only half of the Scotch eggs, turn the balls over after 2 to 3 minutes. If you see any starting to burn, turn them over immediately. Cook for another 3 to 4 minutes or until golden brown.

8   While the Scotch eggs are cooking, prepare the sauce by combining the gochujang, mayo, and lemon juice. Mix well.

9   Remove the Scotch eggs from the oil once they are evenly cooked to a golden-brown exterior. Allow them to cool on a drying rack.

10 Cut the Scotch eggs in half to expose the cross section of the egg. The yolk should still be runny.

11 Spoon the sauce onto a small plate, and place half a Scotch egg on top. Garnish with green onion and ikura, if using.

7 eggs, divided
2 cups (120g) panko
⅔ cup (80g) cornstarch
2lb (900g) salmon filet, minced or scraped off the bone
1 tsp (7g) kosher salt
1 tsp (3g) cracked black pepper
1 tsp (3g) smoked paprika
4 cups (1L) canola oil
¼ cup (60ml) gochujang or hot sauce
¼ cup (60ml) Kewpie mayo
Juice of ½ lemon
½ bunch of green onions, thinly sliced (optional), to garnish
¼ cup (50g) ikura (optional), to garnish

Note
Experiment using various starches to achieve different crunchy textures. Mochiko will provide a very good crunch with added chewiness.

Scan for bonus content.

Blueberry-Cured Salmon

serves **4** | prep **15 minutes, plus 7 hours to marinate** | cook **None**

In the summertime, there is an overlap of seasons: wild salmon and wild blueberry seasons. Those two things might not seem like a good combination, but there is absolutely a way to make it delicious. For instance, this recipe takes sweet and tart blueberries and uses them to cure salmon. Since this recipe involves eating salmon raw, it is important to follow the "Preparing Fish for Sashimi" section (see page 23).

1 In a medium bowl, combine the salt and sugar and mix well.

2 Spread some of the salt-and-sugar mix in an even layer on a baking sheet. Place the salmon filet on top and coat with the rest of the salt and sugar. Refrigerate for 1 hour to cure.

3 With a paper towel, lightly wipe off the salt and sugar from the filet. It's okay for some to remain on the salmon.

4 Using a spoon or brush, coat the salmon with the honey. Then, evenly sprinkle on the kaffir lime leaves and chili flakes.

5 Place the filet in a resealable plastic bag, and add the blueberries. Refrigerate for 6 to 8 hours.

6 Remove the filet from the plastic bag and pat dry with a paper towel. If you don't want all the kaffir lime leaves and chili flakes remaining on the filet, rinse the salmon under cold water and pat dry.

7 Using a sharp knife, slice the filet into thin pieces for serving. Enjoy with thinly sliced red onion and microgreens, if desired.

2 cups (450g) kosher salt

2 cups (400g) granulated sugar

2lb (900g) salmon filet

2 tbsp (30ml) honey

2 kaffir lime leaves, finely chopped, or lime zest if unavailable

1 tbsp (7g) chili flakes

1 cup (150g) blueberries, blended or crushed

Scan for bonus content.

Salmon Carpaccio

serves **2–4** | prep **20 minutes** | cook **None**

There are multiple names for a dish featuring raw fish: sashimi, carpaccio, crudo, etc. The way I see it, these names all pretty much mean the same thing. I describe this specific recipe as "carpaccio," because carpaccio commonly uses thinly sliced meat topped with olive oil, lemon, and other ingredients. To cut the salmon into thin slices, I recommend a yanagiba knife (see page 15). There are endless combinations of ingredients you can use for this dish, but one of my favorite flavor pairings with salmon is sesame oil and sea salt.

1 Use the green portion of the green onion, and with a sharp knife, butterfly the green onion. Slice into 2-inch (5cm) segments. Stack the segments and thinly slice lengthwise. Add the sliced green onion to an ice bath for at least 10 minutes.

2 Spread the salmon slices neatly across a cutting board. To the middle of each piece of salmon, add 1 to 2 slices of shallot. Roll the salmon around the shallot, creating a neat roll. Transfer the salmon to a serving dish and top with the green onion, sesame oil, sesame seeds, lemon zest, and sea salt. Sprinkle with lemon juice just before serving.

2 green onions

8oz (225g) salmon filet, thinly sliced in ¼-in (6mm) strips

½ shallot, thinly sliced vertically with the grain

1 tbsp (15ml) sesame oil

Pinch of sesame seeds

Zest of 1 lemon

Pinch of flaky sea salt

1 tsp lemon juice, to serve

Salmon Collar Ochazuke
(Rice Tea Soup)

serves **4** | prep **5 minutes** | cook **20 minutes**

This one is inspired by a childhood favorite of mine, ochazuke. It's a common, quick Japanese meal. Genmaicha, a type of green tea made with roasted rice, is poured over a bowl of rice and toppings and served as a soup. The dish is light, flavorful, versatile, and quick to make. The easiest way to prepare it is by using an ochazuke packet, which are typically located in the Asian-ingredients aisle of your supermarket: simply add it to a bowl of rice and fill the bowl with tea. This is a more refined version of the dish using salmon collar.

1 Preheat the oven or grill to 450°F (230°C).

2 Place the rice in a medium pot and level it so it sits perfectly flat. Use your index finger as a guideline and place it so your fingertip touches the top of the rice. Add water to the pot until it reaches just under your first knuckle. Add the soy sauce. Salt the salmon filet, and place it in the pot.

3 Cover the pot with a lid, and place the pot over high heat. Start a timer for 20 minutes. When the water comes to a boil, reduce the heat to low. Keep on low heat until the timer expires. Take the pot off the heat and let it rest, covered, for 10 minutes, to finish cooking. Once the rice is done cooking, fluff and mix the rice while flaking the salmon.

4 While the rice is cooking, generously salt the salmon collar, then cook in the oven or on the grill for 3 to 5 minutes on each side, depending on the size of the collar.

5 In a saucepan, brew 8 cups (2L) of genmaicha as directed on the packaging.

6 Divide the salmon-rice mixture evenly among 4 bowls. Sprinkle each serving with furikake. Pour 1½ to 2 cups (260–480ml) genmaicha over the rice in each bowl. Place a piece of grilled collar in each bowl. Add any desired toppings, and enjoy.

2 cups (400g) medium-grain white rice, rinsed
2 tsp (10ml) soy sauce
Salt, to taste
1lb (450g) salmon filet
4 pieces salmon collar
4 tea bags of genmaicha or regular green tea
4 tsp (10g) furikake (Japanese rice seasoning)

Optional toppings
Umeboshi
Green onion
Kombu
Chili crisp
Ikura

Campfire-Smoked Salmon

serves **10–12** | prep **2 hours** | cook **3–6 hours**

I love nothing more than sitting at camp and cooking and eating all day long. One of my favorite camp cooking projects is smoking a whole salmon. It takes a lot of time, but when you're in the great outdoors with no reception, you'll realize you have plenty of time to chill and take your mind off of everything that's happening so you can focus on smoking salmon. The end result is always worth the effort. In my opinion, everybody should try it at least once.

To smoke a salmon using this method, you'll need a baking sheet, a bushcraft knife, twine, and a fire pit and coals. You'll also need wood sticks to create a holder for the salmon. I've found the best wood to use is alder, and there are alder trees all along the Pacific Coast of the US. The main stick should be thick enough to support the weight of the salmon, about 2 inches (5cm) in diameter and at least 3 feet (1m) long. Make sure to choose a stick that's as straight as possible. Lastly, you'll need 6 to 8 smaller sticks, about 1 inch (2.5cm) in diameter, all slightly longer than the width of the salmon. If you don't have access to alder or prefer to use a different wood, you can also go for oak or fruit woods like cherry, apple, or maple. Avoid pine as it contains too much resin and sap, which will leave an unpleasant taste on the meat. Some say pine can be poisonous as well and make people sick. Also avoid conifers like spruce, redwood, fir, and cypress. Cedar planks are often used to smoke salmon on, but be sure to avoid burning cedar wood for the smoke.

For the ingredients, I prefer to use the Diamond Crystal brand for kosher salt, as it's much harder to oversalt using larger crystals with a nonuniform structure to each grain. If you use regular table salt, you'll want to adjust the ratio of salt to sugar so it's 2 parts salt to 3 parts sugar (instead of 1 part salt to 1 part sugar). It's also important to remember that 75 percent of wild salmon contains parasites, so if the salmon you're using was wild caught, don't forget the crucial last step to ensure all parasites are killed.

This method of smoking is the way Native Americans have been smoking salmon for hundreds of years. You can still witness this technique in certain tribes such as the Makah in Neah Bay, Washington. I was there for Makah Days, an annual celebration of Native American culture. They were smoking 2 to 3 dozen salmon at a time! You can make all sorts of dishes with smoked salmon. Eat it on its own, or make bagels, fried rice, or the smoked salmon dip recipe on page 83.

1 whole salmon, 8–12lb (3.6–5.4kg)
1lb (450g) kosher salt
1lb (450g) granulated sugar

1   Starting with a whole salmon, cut off the head and butterfly the entire fish. Remove the rib cage and pin bones.

2   Mix the salt and sugar together, then evenly spread a generous amount on a baking sheet. Lay the salmon skin side down on top of the salt and sugar. Sprinkle the rest of the salt-and-sugar mixture over the meat so that the salmon is buried in salt and sugar, a process called dry brining. For a 10-pound (4.5kg) salmon, allow the meat to brine for 2 hours, adding 15 minutes for every additional 2 pounds. After the brining process, wash the salt and sugar off with cold water and pat dry.

3   While the salmon is dry brining, make a holder for the salmon. Using a bushcraft knife or pocketknife, split the stick in the middle about halfway down. It's easiest to hit the tip of the knife with another stick while pushing down on the handle. Insert the split all the way into the salmon headfirst, leaving a filet on either side of the stick. The tail should be at the top of the split. Take the 6 to 8 smaller sticks, and wedge them in on both sides of the salmon, 3 to 4 sticks on each side. You may have to adjust the size of the sticks so they fit snugly in the split. Tie the top of the split together with twine. If the salmon slips down when you hold it up, cut a small slit toward the tail, insert a small stick, and tie that to the top of the split. Now, you should hopefully have something similar to the picture on the next page.

4 When the salmon has dry brined and been patted dry and you've finished constructing the salmon holder, it's time to smoke it. Start by creating a small fire in your fire pit. If you have access to more alder wood, cut it into 6-inch (15cm) pieces and shave off the bark. Place 3 to 4 of those pieces on the hot coals to create a nice smoke.

5 Place the salmon close enough to ensure it makes contact with the smoke. If needed, use additional Y-shaped sticks to create a tripod to hold the salmon stick in the desired spot. Allow the salmon to smoke for at least 3 hours, but up to 6 hours. Why so long? It's unlikely the salmon will make contact with the smoke at all times due to external factors like wind. The less wind, the better. Tend to the sticks often to create a lot of smoke and little to no fire. Sometimes the sticks will catch fire, and adjustments will need to be made, or the smoking wood will need to be replaced with fresh ones. You can create a teepee structure around the smoke and the salmon to block out the wind and keep the smoke in.

6 If using wild-caught salmon, after the 3-to-6-hour smoking process, the salmon will need to be brought up to an internal temperature of 145°F (63°C) to kill potential parasites, as the smoke alone is usually not enough to achieve that. Stoke the fire back up to a medium heat. Lay the salmon horizontally skin-side up just above the fire for 10 to 15 minutes. Flip the salmon and let sit over the fire for another 10 to 15 minutes. If you can pull the meat away from the skin with ease, it is cooked through.

Note
Smoked salmon can last at least 2 weeks refrigerated—but in my experience, it's never actually lasted that long before it's all eaten!

Scan for bonus content.

Smoked Salmon Dip

serves **6–8** | prep **15 minutes** | cook **None**

One of my favorite snacks to eat while fishing is smoked salmon dip. For some unknown reason, I always have good luck when I eat smoked salmon while fishing. As a fisherman, I live by this quote from Michael Scott from *The Office:* "I'm not superstitious, but I am a little-stitious." So, this dish has become my good luck charm. This recipe will work with any smoked fish, but if it's not salmon, you'll be pushing your luck.

1 In a large bowl, combine all the ingredients. To get the perfect spice balance, mix all the ingredients together, adding as little or as much wasabi as you'd like. Taste and adjust accordingly.

2 Enjoy with your favorite crackers!

1lb (450g) smoked salmon, chopped

Two 8oz (227g) blocks cream cheese, softened to room temperature

1 cup (250g) plain Greek yogurt

1–2 tbsp (15–30ml) wasabi, to taste

1½ bunches of green onion, chopped

1 serrano pepper, chopped

1 tbsp (15ml) light soy sauce

Note

The cream cheese will take about 30 minutes to 1 hour to soften to room temperature. Alternatively, you can microwave it in a glass bowl for 30 seconds. The fat from the cream cheese helps to dilute the spice of the wasabi, so you can be generous with the amount of wasabi you use!

Ikura (Marinated Salmon Roe)

makes **about 14 ounces (400g)** | prep **20 minutes** | cook **None**

Ikura is the Japanese word for salmon roe. The biggest and best roe comes from chum salmon, aka dog salmon or keta salmon, but all salmon roe is edible. Roe can be harvested in the summer and fall and is usually at its best before salmon start spawning. Once the salmon go upriver to spawn, their roe starts to get firm. You can still eat it, but it becomes difficult to bite down on, as it slips between your teeth and gets hard to pop.

Many parts of the West Coast have salmon hatcheries where the eggs are manually fertilized and hatched and where salmon stay in freshwater for up to a year. This gives the salmon a much higher chance of survival. Before they're released into the wild, the adipose fin is clipped to mark that it's a hatchery fish.

These hatchery fish are caught by all types of fishermen. They are completely wild and allow for sustainable fishery. Some hatchery programs release fish remotely, away from the hatchery, meaning that when the salmon come back to spawn, they will have nowhere to go and are unable to lay their eggs. These fish are placed to stimulate the fishery. So don't feel bad for keeping a female salmon with roe.

If your local fishmonger carries salmon, ask them if they have "skein," which is the term for the salmon egg sack. (Female salmon have two sacks each.) Then, you don't have to even catch any salmon! Many fishermen save the skein for bait. It is one of the best forms of bait to catch salmon or steelheads heading upriver to spawn. I usually keep a little for bait and save the rest to eat.

This is my preferred method to separate the roe from the skein. I then marinate my ikura, and it always comes out amazing. One of my favorite foods of all time.

1 To make the marinade, in a small bowl or jar, combine the dashi, usukuchi soy sauce, mirin, and yuzu extract. Refrigerate until ready to use.

2 Place 1 whole sack of roe into a large bowl. Pour boiling water over it, filling the bowl. Using a pair of chopsticks, lightly agitate the egg sack. The individual pieces of roe will begin falling off the skein. Continue the process until the roe is fully separated from the sack. Discard the clump of skein.

3 Gently pour out the dirty water. Rinse the roe under cold water. Repeat multiple times to clean out all impurities. During this process, remove bits of skein, popped roe, and anything else that is not fully intact roe. The more time you spend on this process, the better the end result will be. This step should take 10 to 15 minutes.

4 Gently transfer the clean roe into a jar or container. Add the marinade. Cover and refrigerate for at least 2 hours. Ikura will keep for up to 2 weeks in the fridge, but be sure to strain out the marinade after 3 days or it will become too tart.

¾ cup (175ml) dashi
4 tbsp (60ml) usukuchi soy sauce (light-colored soy sauce)
2 tbsp (30ml) mirin
2 tsp (10ml) yuzu extract
1lb (450g) salmon roe with skein (from 1 king salmon)

Scan for bonus content.

Wahoo

A fish so good the Hawaiians named it ono, which directly translates to "tasty," "good," or "delicious." They really are such a delicious fish and a completely versatile meat. It can be grilled, seared, breaded, and even eaten raw. Wahoo are a pelagic species, making them safe to eat raw straight out of the water. If eating raw, be sure to use best practices when preparing to avoid cross contamination of bacteria.

Wahoo are caught in warm, tropical and subtropical waters like those in Hawaii, the South Pacific Islands, Central America, and even down in New Zealand. They can be caught from boats while trolling at higher speeds or on jigs. Wahoo are tricky to catch because of their incredibly sharp teeth, which can cut through a 100-pound-rated (45kg) monoline with ease. It's best to use at least 12 inches (30cm) of stainless steel wire when targeting wahoo.

Wahoo are closely related to king mackerel and Spanish mackerel, and the following recipes can be done with any of these fish. From my experience serving customers at sushi counters, I've learned some people are put off by the name "mackerel." A typical mackerel refers to "saba," a smaller bait fish with tiger stripes on its back. King and Spanish mackerel are not in the same direct family as those kinds of mackerel, although they are like cousins. Saba is known to be a stronger-tasting fish and gets described as being "fishy." Wahoo, king mackerel, and Spanish mackerel are not fishy or strong-tasting. So for people who do not like regular mackerel, I guarantee you will still love wahoo, king mackerel, and Spanish mackerel.

Cold-Smoked Wahoo Sashimi

serves **10–12** | prep **25 minutes** | cook **5 minutes**

My favorite preparation for wahoo is lightly smoked. This recipe is one that used to blow people's minds at the sushi bar. It's a simple-looking piece of fish with a huge depth of flavor that requires a technique called "dry brine," where you bury the meat in salt and sugar. The skin is seared using a blow torch or broiler for added smokiness and char. Then it is lightly smoked and wrapped in plastic wrap to seal in the smoke. I like to create a makeshift cold smoker using two metal hotel pans (what you see in buffet lines holding food) and a wire rack. I put smoking wood chips like cherry or apple wood in one corner of the hotel pan and place that corner over a gas burner to create the smoke. Alternatively, you can use two stainless steel mixing bowls of the same size. Put woodchips in the bottom of one, then the filet on a grill rack placed between another mixing bowl faced down to create a dome.

1   In a medium bowl, combine the salt and sugar. Mix well so each scoop has equal amounts of both salt and sugar.

2   Cover the bottom of a baking sheet with less than half of the salt-and-sugar mixture, making sure it's spread out evenly.

3   Place the filet skin side down onto the baking sheet. Cover the entire filet with the rest of the salt-and-sugar mixture. Be generous with the amount you put on top. The filet should look almost buried. Refrigerate for 45 minutes.

4   Rinse the fish in cold water, removing all the salt and sugar, and pat dry.

5   Sear the skin with a blow torch until it has a good char. Make sure the skin side is facing the heat source and be careful not to cook the actual meat.

6   Shape a 10 x 10-inch (25 x 25cm) sheet of foil into a bowl and add the wood chips.

7   Place the foil bowl with the wood chips in one corner of a hotel pan. Set the pan on the stove over medium heat so that the wood chips are directly above the flame. The wood chips will soon begin to smoke.

8   Place the filet on a wire rack, then set the wire rack between the hotel pans to smoke. Turn off the stove as the smoke gets thick. If the smoke turns from white to yellow, immediately turn the stove off. Leave the filet in the smoke for 5 minutes.

9   Remove the filet from the smoke and enfold in plastic wrap. Leave it in the wrap for at least 30 minutes before slicing into sashimi pieces.

10 Serve as sashimi with ponzu and wasabi or as nigiri. Daikon oroshi is also another good topping for this dish.

2 cups (450g) kosher salt

2 cups (400g) granulated sugar

4lb (1.8kg) boneless wahoo filet, skin on

1 cup (90g) smoking wood chips (cherry, apple, mesquite, or even coconut husk)

Optional toppings

Ponzu

Wasabi

Daikon oroshi

Note
Keep the filet as far away from the fire source so as not to cook the fish. This specific technique is to cold smoke the filet.

Scan for bonus content.

Coconut Cream Wahoo

serves **4–6** | prep **20 minutes** | cook **5 minutes**

I've spent this past year in some of the most beautiful tropical islands in the South Pacific, like Niue and Samoa. It's what you imagine when you think of paradise—big fish and coconuts! A delicious recipe I've learned in my time there is a coconut cream wahoo dish called ota. It's simple yet delicious, especially if you have access to fresh coconuts. This dish is essentially the tropical island version of ceviche.

1 In a large bowl, combine the cubed fish and lime juice. Let sit for 5 minutes.

2 Add the cherry tomatoes, cucumbers, shallots or red onion, green onions, coconut cream, and chili peppers, if using. Mix well.

3 In a medium pan, heat the cooking oil over medium heat. Add the taro and cook until lightly brown, 5 to 6 minutes. Transfer the taro chips to a baking sheet lined with a paper towel or a wire rack to cool.

4 Serve the fish in a bowl with the taro chips on the side.

2lb (900g) skinless, boneless wahoo filet, cut into ½-in (1.2cm) cubes

Juice of 2 limes

10–15 cherry tomatoes, halved or quartered

1 cup (130g) diced cucumber

¼ cup (30g) diced shallots or red onion

¼ cup (10g) sliced green onions

2 cups (500ml) fresh coconut cream or 1 can (400ml) coconut milk

1–5 pieces spicy chili pepper, like habanero or serrano (optional)

¼ cup (60ml) cooking oil (canola, vegetable, etc.)

1lb (450g) taro, peeled and thinly sliced

Note
This dish is specifically great with wahoo but can be done with any fish suitable for raw consumption.

Scan for bonus content.

Grilled Wahoo
with Coconut Garlic Rice

serves **4–6** | prep **6 minutes** | cook **25 minutes**

Most fish are either delicate and flaky or dense and firm. Wahoo is on the firm side of the spectrum, which makes it a great fish for grilling. In this recipe, it is simply grilled and served with a side of coconut garlic rice.

Keep in mind that the easiest way to ruin a good piece of fish is by overcooking it. Fish cooks much faster than steak—if you wait until you think it's done, it should've been off the heat a full minute ago! Aim to undercook just slightly (medium to medium-rare finish) and let the residual heat finish the job.

1 Preheat a grill to 400°F (200°C). Prepare the fish for grilling by seasoning generously with salt.

2 While the grill heats, prepare the rice. In a dry 10-inch (25cm) skillet over medium-low heat, toast the shredded coconut for 5 minutes or until lightly brown.

3 In a medium pot, combine the toasted coconut, washed rice, coconut milk, garlic, 1 cup (250ml) water, and a pinch of salt. Bring to a boil over high heat. Once boiling, reduce the heat to low and simmer for 12 minutes. Turn off the heat and let rest for 10 minutes. Before serving, stir in the butter and fluff the rice with a fork.

4 Place the fish on the grill and cook for 7 minutes on each side, making sure to sear the skin as well. It's better to undercook fish rather than overcook it, as it can become tough and dry. To test for doneness, use a butter knife to peek into the center of the fish. If the meat slides off the bone with ease, it's cooked. Remove the fish from the grill as soon as it's cooked through.

5 To serve, plate the fish and rice and garnish with chives.

1lb (450g) wahoo, skin on
2 tsp (12g) salt, plus more to taste
½ cup (50g) shredded coconut
2 cups (400g) medium-grain white rice, rinsed
1 can (400ml) coconut milk
8 garlic cloves, chopped
2 tbsp (28g) butter
Chopped chives, to garnish

Halibut

The California halibut is often fished from kayaks and boats in the San Francisco Bay Area. They are caught in many areas of the bay around San Francisco, Tiburon, Treasure Island, and more. The easiest method is to troll frozen herring just off the bottom at 1.5 to 3 miles per hour (2.5–5kph). Another effective method is to drift live bait about 1 foot (30cm) off the bottom. There is no official season for halibut, but the bite picks up in the spring and throughout the summer. It is a very beginner-friendly fish for anybody looking to get into fishing on kayaks or boats.

Comparing California Halibut and Pacific Halibut

	California halibut	Pacific halibut
Physical features	• Round shape • Light to dark brown with some light and dark spots • Can weigh between 5 and 20 pounds (2–9kg), with a record weight of 72 pounds (32.5kg)	• Diamond shape • Brownish to dark green with light and dark spots • Can weigh between 5 and 100 pounds (2–45kg), with a record weight of 459 pounds (208kg)
Flavor and Texture	• Flaky and firm • Medium density • Mild flavor, takes on other flavors well • Juicy but easily overcooked and can dry out	• Firm • Medium density • Clean flavor with a light brine • Stays juicy and moist a bit longer than California halibut

Scan for bonus content.

Halibut Sisig

serves **4–5** | prep **15 minutes** | cook **30 minutes**

During college, I lived in Daly City, California, and if you know anything about the area, you know there's a lot of fog and a huge population of Filipino people. I quickly learned that Filipino food is delicious, and one of my favorites is sisig. It's typically made with many parts of the pig, including the cheeks, ear, snout, liver, and belly. This dish can also be made with most kinds of fish, but I like to use halibut, as it has firm, flaky meat.

1 Heat a large cast-iron or carbon-steel pan over medium-high heat for 3 to 4 minutes. Once hot, 1 tablespoon oil. Season the halibut filets generously with salt and pepper on each side, then add the halibut filets to the pan. Cook for 3 to 4 minutes on each side, depending on the thickness. Once cooked through, remove from the heat and let cool. Break apart the meat in small flakes, and set aside.

2 If using the fish skin, liver, engawa, and stomach: To the same pan over medium heat, add 1 tablespoon oil. Add the fish skin, and cook for 4 to 5 minutes or until crispy. Remove the skin from the pan, and set aside. Add the fish liver, engawa, and fish stomach. Cook for 4 to 6 minutes, or until fully cooked. Remove from the pan, slice the liver into bite-size pieces, and set aside.

3 In the same pan, add the remaining 2 tablespoons oil. Add the chopped onion and flaked halibut, and cook for 2 to 3 minutes. Next, add the chopped garlic, chili peppers, engawa, and stomach. Mix together and cook for another minute. Add the butter, Kewpie mayo, soy sauce, and rice vinegar. Cook for an additional 2 to 3 minutes or until a crispy layer has formed on the bottom. Add the sliced red onion, mix, and remove from the heat.

4 Onto a serving plate, scoop a generous serving of the sisig, then the crispy fish skin, sliced fish liver, green onion, fried garlic, egg yolk, and a squeeze of lime.

¼ cup (60ml) cooking oil, divided
2lb (900g) halibut filet, skin removed and reserved
1 tbsp (18g) salt
1 tsp (3g) black pepper
¼ cup (30g) fish skin (optional)
1 halibut liver, whole (optional)
½lb (225g) engawa (fin muscle) (optional)
1 halibut stomach, chopped (optional)
¼ cup (30g) chopped yellow onion
4–6 garlic cloves, chopped
1–2 chili, habanero, serrano, or jalapeño peppers, diced
2 tbsp (28g) unsalted butter
1 tbsp (15ml) Kewpie mayo
1½ tsp (7.5ml) soy sauce
1½ tsp (7.5ml) rice vinegar
¼ red onion, sliced
½ cup (50g) chopped green onion
1 tbsp (6g) fried garlic
1 egg yolk
1 lime, quartered

Scan for bonus content.

Blackened Halibut Tacos
with Avocado Salsa

serves **2–4** | prep **10 minutes** | cook **15 minutes**

In San Francisco Bay, one of the most common fish to target is California halibut. The best bite is in the spring from March to June. Kayak fishing is very effective for catching California halibut, especially using live bait. I like to catch my own live bait with a cast net, usually small jack smelt. Otherwise, frozen herring works well. Halibut can be caught at many of the piers in the SF Bay, two hours before and after high tide or low tide. They tend to bite more when the tides are small.

This is the perfect summer fish taco recipe, with blackened halibut paired with Jocelyn's avocado salsa. Blackening seasoning is just a bunch of different seasonings combined to make one tasty, smoky, spicy blend. You can buy premade blackening seasoning, but most likely you already have everything you need to make your own. I suggest my own blend of seasonings below, but feel free to add more according to your taste and preferences, like dry lemon zest for a kick of acidity or dried shallots for more sweetness.

1 To make the blackening seasoning, in a small bowl, whisk together all of the ingredients. Transfer to a small jar for storage and future use.

2 To make the tacos, season the halibut strips generously on all sides with the blackening seasoning. Set aside.

3 In a blender, combine the avocados, jalapeños, a handful of cilantro (making sure to save some for garnish), the lime juice (more or less according to your taste preference), garlic cloves, serranos, salt, and 1 tablespoon (15ml) water. Blend thoroughly until the salsa is smooth. Set aside until ready to serve.

4 In a large skillet or on a flat-top grill over medium heat, heat 1 tablespoon (15ml) oil and spread it around the entire surface. Add the onion and cook for 5 to 6 minutes.

5 Push the onion to one side of the pan. Add the remaining 1 tablespoon (15ml) oil and the seasoned halibut, being careful not to overcrowd the pan. It's best to leave at least 1 inch (2.5cm) of space between each piece of halibut. Cook for 3 to 4 minutes on one side. Flip and cook for another 3 minutes. Remove from the pan immediately and place on a plate or baking sheet.

6 In a medium skillet over medium heat, heat the tortillas 2 to 3 at a time. Assemble the tacos by placing halibut, grilled onion, and salsa on a tortilla. Squeeze some lime juice over top, and garnish with reserved cilantro.

For the seasoning
1 tbsp (9g) smoked paprika
2 tsp (2g) cayenne pepper
1 tbsp (10g) garlic powder
1 tbsp (9g) onion powder
1 tbsp (9g) black pepper
½ tsp (1g) dried oregano
½ tbsp (3g) dried thyme
1 tbsp (18g) salt

For the tacos
2lb (900g) halibut filet, cut into strips 1in (2.5cm) thick and 3–4in (7–10cm) long
2 ripe avocados
4 jalapeños
1 bunch of cilantro, divided
Juice from 2–3 limes
4 garlic cloves
2 serrano peppers
1 tsp (6g) salt
2 tbsp (30ml) cooking oil, divided
1 yellow onion, sliced into rings
Twelve 6-in (15cm) corn tortillas

Scan for bonus content.

Tuna

Tuna are a large species of fish commonly found in deeper water. A few species like bluefin, yellowfin, and big eye tuna can reach hundreds of pounds. There are also smaller varieties of tuna, including albacore and bonito. All of these species of tuna can be caught in the Pacific Ocean. Out of all the tuna species, bonito are the easiest to catch and are often caught off piers in southern California with jigs, lures, or bait. The yellowfin tuna is commonly caught offshore in southern California and Baja using jigs and lures. Albacore tuna are cold water tuna and more commonly caught further north, starting from just offshore the San Francisco Bay Area and up to Washington. High-speed trolling, using cedar plugs and other trolling lures, is the most common method of catching albacore.

In recent years, the mighty bluefin tuna have been consistently fished 30 to 60 miles (50–100km) offshore around the San Francisco Bay Area. Although bluefin tuna have been considered unsustainable in the past, they have made a remarkable return in high numbers. It is not uncommon to catch 100- to 200-pound (45–90kg) bluefin tuna around San Francisco, but they are far from easy to catch. The most commonly used fishing method in that area is trolling high-speed lures like Madmacs. Other effective methods are slow trolling live bait, such as mackerel and sardines, or dropping 200- to 400-gram vertical jigs.

I am far from a professional tuna fisherman. I have been on the hunt for tuna in the Bay Area at least seven times and have only managed to catch two fish, and both of those fish were on the same day. After I finally managed to catch a bluefin tuna, I decided to share my catch with the community. I showed up to Pacifica Pier, a popular fishing pier in the Bay Area, and sliced fresh-caught bluefin tuna for free to anybody that came.

Bluefin Tuna Carpaccio with Olives and Chili Crisp

serves **2–3** | prep **15 minutes** | cook **None**

This dish makes for a great appetizer. Bluefin tuna has 3 main cuts: akami (red or lean meat), chutoro (medium fatty meat) and o-toro (fatty meat). Akami holds the essence of the tuna, whereas o-toro, with its rich and fatty quality, simply melts in your mouth. I prefer chutoro, because it's the best of both worlds—flavorful without being too fatty. Using the chutoro cut will give the carpaccio a mix of fatty and lean parts to enjoy. It breaks apart easily, so serve with chopsticks or a fork.

1   Wrap the cuts of tuna with plastic wrap. Using a tortilla press, gently smash the tuna into a thin layer about ⅛ inch (3mm) thick. If you don't have a tortilla press, use a rolling pin or wine bottle. The tuna should flatten to about 5 times the original surface area.

2   Slap the thin layer of tuna onto a plate. Garnish with the rest of the ingredients, being generous with the oil of the kelp chili crisp.

12oz (350g) bluefin tuna, sliced into ½-in (1.2cm) cuts

2 tbsp (30ml) kelp chili crisp, plus oil

8 olives

2 small cherry belle radishes, thinly sliced

¼ red onion, thinly sliced

Handful of microgreens

Zest of 1 lemon

½ tsp (3g) flaky sea salt

Ginger Poke with Popped Rice

serves **2** | prep **15 minutes** | cook **None**

One of my favorite poke dishes I've had was the ginger poke in Oahu. You can use any fish that is suitable for raw consumption for this recipe, but the best is ahi, aka yellowfin tuna. I was messing around with the idea of eating poke with crunchy rice, which is in no way traditional, but it works great. The easiest way to make crunchy or popped rice is to use parboiled rice, the type advertised as "microwave ready in 2 minutes." It can be bought in most supermarkets. If using regular rice, it would need to be boiled, then dehydrated, which takes a lot of time. Using parboiled rice allows you to go straight to the popping step.

1   To a small saucepan over medium heat, add 1 tablespoon canola oil and the sesame oil. Heat for 1 minute, then add the ginger, garlic, honey, and salt. Cook for 2 minutes, mixing frequently. Add the sliced green onions and remove from the heat and transfer to a small bowl. Allow the sauce to cool to room temperature, and set aside.

2   In a medium-to-large pan warmed over medium heat, add the remaining 1 tablespoon canola oil and wait for it to heat up. Open the parboiled rice pack and break apart the grains into a bowl. Then add 1 cup (94g) parboiled rice to the hot oil and cover with a lid. It will immediately start to pop and sizzle in the hot oil. Try to separate the grains of rice as it cooks using chopsticks or a long spoon. Cook for approximately 8 minutes, and once it stops popping, transfer the rice into a sieve and set aside. Repeat for the rest of the rice.

3   In a medium bowl, combine the sauce from step one, and the ahi. Mix in the sesame seeds and lemon zest.

4   In a small serving bowl, add a scoop of the crunchy rice and place the ginger ahi on top!

2 tbsp (15ml) canola oil, divided
1 tbsp (15ml) sesame oil
1½ tbsp (23g) grated ginger
1½ tbsp (23g) grated garlic
2 tsp (10ml) honey
½ tsp (3g) salt
1 bunch of green onions, sliced
2 cups (188g) parboiled rice
1lb (450g) ahi (yellowfin tuna) filet, sliced into 1in cubes
½ tbsp (5g) sesame seeds
Zest of 1 lemon

Tuna Zuke (Marinated Tuna)

makes **10–12 pieces of nigiri** | prep **10 minutes, plus 1 hour to marinate** | cook **1 minute**

Zuke is a marinated piece of tuna that you might see at high-end sushi restaurants. A piece of tuna saku is blanched, then marinated in soy sauce. It works with any tuna, but it's best with bluefin tuna, chutoro (medium fatty bluefin). Wrap the block of tuna in a paper towel to ensure the entire piece of meat gets marinated evenly without submerging it entirely in soy sauce. As the paper towel absorbs the marinade, it spreads it across the saku block.

1 Bring a medium pot of water to a boil over high heat. Using tongs, place the tuna block into the boiling water for 3 seconds. Immediately remove from the boiling water and place into an ice bath. Pat dry with paper towels.

2 Add the soy sauce and mirin to a large zipperlock bag. Wrap the tuna with a paper towel, making sure the tuna is completely covered. Place the towel-wrapped tuna into the bag with the marinade. Let marinate in the fridge for at least 1 hour, and up to 8 hours, before use.

3 Remove the tuna from the marinade and pat dry with paper towels. With a sharp knife, slice the tuna into sashimi or nigiri pieces.

4 With a blow torch, sear the fatty side of the nigiri. Garnish with chili paste and chives.

10–12oz (300–350g) block bluefin tuna

½ cup (125ml) soy sauce

2 tbsp (30ml) mirin

1 tsp (6g) yuzu kosho or chili paste

1 bunch of chives, cut into 1-in (2.5cm) pieces

Albacore Tuna Sashimi

serves **4–6** | prep **10 minutes** | cook **2 minutes**

Albacore tuna is another sustainable seafood. They don't grow big like the yellowfin or bluefin, but they are extremely delicious. It has a pinkish-white flesh, and is sometimes referred to as white tuna or shiromaguro. It's a bit softer than the typical yellowfin and has good fat content for its size. It is an underrated species of tuna that deserves tons of love. Sushi restaurants prepare it simply by blanching or searing quartered loins of filet to firm up the exterior. Albacore tuna can be caught in many parts of the world. On the West Coast of the US, it is caught anywhere from California to Washington, usually 30 miles (48km) or more offshore.

1 Place the albacore on a metal sheet pan or cedar plank. Use a flame torch to sear the fish on all sides. The pinkish white flesh will turn bright white with spots of char. This takes approximately 30 seconds per side. Using a sharp knife, slice the albacore into ¼-inch (6mm) sashimi, and set aside.

2 In a small bowl, mix the cornstarch and ¼ cup (60ml) cold water to make a slurry.

3 To a small saucepan, add the lemon juice, sugar, cornstarch slurry, and a small pinch of salt. Bring to a simmer over medium-high heat. Once the sauce thickens, remove from the heat. Let cool to room temperature, then add the chives and lemon zest.

4 Arrange the sashimi on a serving dish and drizzle a generous spoonful of sauce over top. Garnish with the cherry tomatoes and microgreens, and enjoy.

1lb (450g) loin of albacore
2 tsp (5g) cornstarch
3 tbsp (45ml) lemon juice
1 tbsp (12g) sugar
Pinch of salt
1 tbsp (3g) chopped chives
Zest of 1 lemon
4–6 cherry tomatoes, quartered
¼ cup (20g) microgreens

Grilled Tuna Collar with Yuzu Kosho

serves **2** | prep **30 minutes** | cook **10 minutes**

In recent years, the bluefin tuna fishery in California has been booming. We've known tuna to be caught in Southern California, but it has now become common for tuna to be caught around Monterey Bay, the Bay Area, Bodega Bay, and even Fort Bragg, typically 20 miles (32km) or more offshore trolling big Madmac lures. It's a pursuit of high risk and high reward. Once you catch a big tuna, one of the first pieces you can cook up is the collar. It holds some of the fattiest meat on the fish and is extremely rich and tasty. A piece of kamatoro (fatty collar) looks like a piece of wagyu beef.

Grilling is an easy and tasty way to prepare the collar. It pairs well with Japanese fermented citrus chili, known as yuzu kosho, which is made by fermenting yuzu (Japanese citrus) with chili peppers and salt. It's easy to make yourself at home. Use any citrus, like lemon, lime, grapefruit, etc. Grate all the zest using a microplane and combine with chopped chili and salt, then ferment for two weeks. One of my favorite combinations is grapefruit and habanero yuzu kosho. It will last for months in the fridge, so making big batches will save you time in the future.

Yuzu Kosho

1 In a small bowl, combine the chopped serrano or habanero peppers with the zest.

2 Weigh the zest-chili mixture, and add 10 percent of that weight in salt. For example, for 100g zest-chili mixture, use 10g salt. Then add the citrus juice and mix well.

3 Transfer the mixture into a small jar or container with a lid, and place in a cool, dark area for two weeks to ferment. Open slightly and reseal the lid every other day to "burp" the fermentation. Taste the fermentation after two weeks; if you're happy with it, transfer it to the refrigerator for storage. Now you have yuzu kosho ready to use anytime!

Grilled Tuna Collar

1 Preheat the grill to 550°F (285°C).

2 In a small bowl, mix together all the dry ingredients. Season the tuna collar generously with the seasoning mixture, then add a coat of oil to the collar.

3 Place the collar on the grill and cook for 4 to 6 minutes on each side, depending on the size of the collar.

4 Once cooked through, place the collar on a plate and enjoy with the yuzu kosho.

For the yuzu kosho

1–2 serrano or habanero peppers, finely chopped

Zest of 5–10 citrus fruits (yuzu, lemon, lime, grapefruit, etc., or a mix)

1–2 tsp (6–12g) salt (equal to 10 percent of the weight of the zest)

2 tbsp (30ml) citrus juice

For the grilled tuna collar

1 tbsp (9g) smoked paprika

1 tsp (3g) black pepper

1 tsp (3g) ginger powder

1 tsp (3g) onion powder

1 tsp (3g) sesame seeds

1 tsp (3g) ground cardamom

1 tsp (6g) salt

2–5lb (1–2kg) tuna collar

2 tbsp (30ml) cooking oil

Miso-Marinated Yellowtail Sashimi

serves **4** | prep **30 minutes, plus 8 hours to marinate** | cook **20 minutes**

Yellowtail, aka hamachi, buri, or kingfish (in New Zealand), can be caught in many parts of the Pacific Ocean, mostly in the subtropical regions. I've caught them in southern California, northern New Zealand, and southern Japan. These fish are very strong and extremely fun to catch. There's also a reason why you see hamachi in just about every sushi restaurant—it's delicious, firm, and has notes of citrus.

1   Place yellowtail blocks on a baking sheet, and sprinkle generously with salt on all sides. Let sit for 20 minutes. Rinse off the salt under cold water, and pat dry with paper towels.

2   Meanwhile, make the marinade. In a medium bowl, combine the miso paste, light soy sauce, mirin, lemon juice, and half of the lemon zest. Mix well. Add the fish, turning to coat with the marinade. Cover and refrigerate for 8 hours.

3   In a small saucepan, heat the canola oil over low heat. When hot, add the green onions, and fry for 20 minutes or until they start to brown. Use a fine mesh strainer to strain out the green onions, reserving the oil. Place the green onions on a paper towel to absorb the oil. Set the fried green onions and reserved oil aside.

4   Using paper towels, wipe the miso marinade off the fish (some miso can remain). With a sharp knife, score the skin (or, if the skin was removed, what would be the skin side). Place the fish on a fireproof surface, like a baking sheet, cast-iron pan, or cedar plank. Using a blow torch, sear the scored area. If you don't have a blow torch, preheat a skillet over high heat, add a touch of oil, then place the fish in the hot pan, skin side down, and hold it for approximately 10 seconds for a proper sear.

5   With a sharp knife, slice the fish into ¼-inch (6mm) slices or thinner. Plate the slices, then top with the fried green onions, reserved green onion oil, microgreens, flaky sea salt, and the remaining lemon zest. Serve fresh.

1lb (450g) yellowtail filet, cut into saku blocks
2 tbsp (36g) salt
½ cup (120g) white miso paste
1 tbsp (15ml) light soy sauce
2 tbsp (30ml) mirin
1½ tbsp (23ml) lemon juice
Zest of 1 lemon, divided
¼ cup (60ml) canola oil
1 bunch of green onions, thinly sliced
¼ cup (20g) microgreens
Pinch of flaky sea salt

Grilled Skin-On Yellowtail with Caper Sauce

serves **4** | prep **15 minutes** | cook **2 hours 15 minutes**

Yellowtail is a highly versatile fish, great in raw preparations as well as grilled. Any chance I get, I like to use the entire fish. This recipe showcases how easy it is to make a stock using the fish head, which contains a lot of collagen (good for skin health), as well as vitamin A, omega-3 fatty acids, iron, zinc, and calcium. Not only are fish heads good for you, but they also have a lot of meat that is extra tender, like the cheeks. I like to pull the meat off the bones and eat it while I'm cooking. You can eat it like me or add the meat to the finished dish. Before cooking the fish heads, be sure to remove the gills and wash away any blood.

1   To make the stock, in a large pot bring 8 cups (2L) water to a boil over high heat. Add the fish head and onion halves. Reduce the heat to low and simmer for 15 minutes. At this point, if you choose to eat the meat off the head, remove the fish head and pluck the meat from the cheeks, the top of the head, and behind the eye sockets, or it will overcook and become dry. Place the bones and the head pieces back into the pot and simmer for another 1½ hours. Set the extra fish head meat aside, or enjoy it as a snack!

2   Strain the stock into a container, and let cool to room temperature. Once it's cooled and the fat has risen to the top, gently lay a paper towel on top of the stock and remove it in a swiping motion to absorb as much of the fat as possible. Discard the paper towel, and set the stock aside or refrigerate until ready to use.

3   Preheat the grill on high or to 400°F (200°C). Separately, preheat a skillet over medium heat. Coat the fish with oil and season generously with blackening seasoning or shichimi togarashi.

4   Place the seasoned fish on the grill. Sear the skin side first for 4 to 5 minutes, then flip and sear the other side for another 4 to 5 minutes, depending on the thickness of the filet. Let rest on a cutting board for at least 5 minutes.

5   To make the sauce, to the preheated skillet, add the butter, shallot, sun-dried tomatoes, chili flakes, capers, thyme, and a few pinches of salt. Cook for 2 to 3 minutes. Add 2 cups (500ml) of the fish head stock. Bring the sauce to a simmer, then turn the heat off.

6   To serve, ladle the sauce into shallow bowls. Place the grilled fish in the sauce, squeeze some lemon juice over top, and garnish with lemon zest and microgreens.

2lb (900g) skin-on yellowtail filet, quartered
1 tbsp (15ml) cooking oil
Blackening seasoning (page 97) or shichimi togarashi
Zest and juice of 1 lemon, for serving
Microgreens, to garnish

For the stock
1 or 2 heads of yellowtail
1 yellow onion, halved

For the sauce
4 tbsp (55g) unsalted butter
1 shallot, minced
Handful of sun-dried tomatoes
1 tsp (3g) chili flakes
3 tbsp (45g) capers
A few sprigs of fresh thyme
Salt, to taste

Note
The stock can be made ahead of time and refrigerated for up to 3 days. The finished dish pairs perfectly with a side of buttered sourdough toast.

Scan for bonus content.

Hawaiian Poke

serves **2–4** | prep **10 minutes** | cook **None**

There is a big difference between poke in Hawaii and poke on the mainland (continental US). In Hawaii, the flavor of the fish is highlighted with complementary flavors, sauces, and minimal ingredients, whereas restaurants on the mainland often add excessive sauces, vegetables, and other ingredients that mask the flavor of the fish. It's much like Japanese sushi versus American sushi. In order to make good poke, all you need are five ingredients besides fish: soy sauce, red or white onion, green onion, sesame seeds, and sesame oil. In addition, you might consider adding chili pepper, sriracha, or chili oil to give it a kick of spice. It is one of the easiest meals to make, and it's a go-to dish with my fresh catch of the day. Make sure to use sushi-grade fish or refer to the section "Safely Enjoying Raw Wild Fish" (see pages 54–55) if using your fresh catch.

1 In a medium bowl, combine the ahi, red or white onion, green onion, soy sauce, sesame oil, and chili crisp. Let the fish marinate for at least 10 minutes, and mix every 1 to 2 minutes. Finish with sesame seeds sprinkled over top.

2 To serve, spoon the poke over steamed rice, if using, and sprinkle with furikake, if desired.

1lb (450g) ahi (yellowfin tuna) filet, sliced into 1-in (2.5cm) cubes

¼ red or white onion, sliced

1 bunch of green onions, sliced

1½ tbsp (23ml) soy sauce

½ tbsp (8ml) sesame oil

1 tbsp (15ml) chili crisp or chili oil

2 tsp (6g) toasted sesame seeds

Steamed white rice (optional), to serve

½ tbsp (5g) furikake (optional), to garnish

Whole Steamed Flounder
with Scallion-Ginger Sauce

serves **2** | prep **15 minutes** | cook **20 minutes**

This recipe works best with pan-size or dinner-plate-size white fish, meaning any fish whose meat is white after it's cooked. Flounder, snapper, and rockfish are all great options. As most white fish have mild-tasting meat, the star of the dish often becomes the sauce. The perfect sauce complements the mild taste of the fish rather than overpowering it. I recommend flounder for this dish, specifically around 2 pounds (900g) in weight. Because flounder have small scales, it's easiest to use a stainless steel sponge to scrub the scales off. You'll need a steamer for this recipe.

1   With a knife, score an X on both sides of the fish. Place it into a steamer (remove the tail of the fish if it is too long to fit into the steamer) and steam for 16 minutes. Check the doneness of the fish by using a fork to gently pull the meat away from the bones. If the meat pulls off easily and cleanly, it is done cooking. Set aside.

2   While the fish is steaming, prepare the sauce. In a small saucepan, heat the canola oil and sesame oil over medium heat. Add the ginger, and cook for 2 minutes, stirring occasionally. Then add the garlic, salt, sugar, and chicken bouillon. Stir for 1 to 2 minutes.

3   When the fish is done steaming, gently remove it from the steamer and set on a plate with a lip to keep the sauce contained.

4   Place the fresh green onion and cilantro on top of the fish. Pour the hot ginger-oil all over the fish. The oil must be hot so the green onion and cilantro sizzle. Serve immediately with a side of rice.

2lb (900g) whole flounder, gutted and scaled
½ cup (125ml) canola oil
1 tbsp (15ml) sesame oil
¼ cup (57g) chopped ginger
4 garlic cloves, chopped
½ tbsp (7g) salt
1 tbsp (15g) brown sugar
2 tsp (8g) chicken bouillon
1 bunch of green onions, chopped
1 bunch of cilantro, roughly chopped

Traditional Snapper Sashimi

makes **25–30 slices** | prep **20 minutes, plus 15 minutes to marinate** | cook **1 minute**

This recipe is the most common way snapper is prepared in sushi restaurants. Snapper (aka mada, tai, madai, and sea bream) holds high value in Japanese culture for its mild and clean flavor that is easy on the palate. It's a great fish to break up stronger-tasting dishes. The texture is delicate, soft, and smooth, creating a pleasant mouthfeel.

This recipe uses a technique called Matsukawa-zukuri, which can be applied to other fish with similar skin and large scales, like sea bass, emperor fish, and hogfish. You'll also have to salt cure the fish, which removes excess water and makes the filet firmer and better able to absorb flavors. Then you'll pour boiling water over the skin; keeping the rib bones attached to the filet prevents the filet from curling when it makes contact with boiling water.

1 Descale, gut, and filet the snapper using the sanmai oroshi technique in the "How to Filet Fish" section (see page 21). Keep the skin and rib cage on.

2 On a baking sheet, evenly sprinkle the salt on both sides of the fish. Let sit for 15 to 20 minutes.

3 In a medium pot, bring 3 cups (750ml) water to a boil over high heat. Place the filet skin-side up on a wire rack in or over the sink. Lay a paper towel on the skin and pour the boiling water over the fish, starting from the tail and moving toward the head. Make sure the boiling water touches all of the skin.

4 Immediately lay the fish skin-side down onto a bed of ice to cool for a minute.

5 Once cooled, remove the rib cage and slice the fish in half lengthwise to cut away the pin bones.

6 With a sharp knife, score the skin 2 to 3 times, lengthwise. Then slice ¼-inch (6mm) pieces at an angle or straight down.

7 Enjoy the sashimi simply with soy sauce and wasabi, or try out the next recipe for something a little different.

4lb (1.8kg) whole snapper
½ tbsp (9g) salt

Scan for bonus content.

Spicy Fried Fish Sandwiches with Onion Rings

serves **2** | prep **15 minutes** | cook **20 minutes**

I love making and eating raw fish dishes, but some days I crave a juicy fried-fish sandwich. This is the perfect meal to hit the spot. Most fish filets will work for this recipe, but the best kinds are fish with dense and meaty flesh, such as lingcod, yellowtail, mahi mahi, halibut, swordfish, and marlin, among many others. This sandwich is inspired by the Nashville hot chicken sandwich, and I think it works great with fish. The tartar sauce and pickled onion suit the fish perfectly and give it a lift of acidity and freshness. For the batter, I like to use a mix of flour and cornstarch, but you can also change things up by replacing the cornstarch with other starches to give it a different texture. Mochiko or glutinous rice flour will give the fish a crunchy and chewy texture. I highly recommend giving this recipe a try.

Onion Rings and Fried Fish

1 Place the fish on a plate or baking sheet and sprinkle about 1 teaspoon salt on each side of each piece of fish for a light salt cure. Refrigerate for 15 minutes. Rinse the fish under cold water and pat dry with a paper towel.

2 In a deep fryer, deep cast-iron skillet, or Dutch oven, heat the canola oil over medium heat to 350°F (180°C).

3 While the oil heats, in a medium bowl, combine the buttermilk and hot sauce. In a second medium bowl, combine the flour, cornstarch, smoked paprika, and onion powder. Mix well.

4 Place the fish and raw onion rings into the buttermilk mixture, turning to ensure all surfaces of the fish and onion rings are evenly coated.

5 Bread and fry the onion rings first. Remove a couple at a time from the buttermilk mixture, dredge with the flour mix, dip back into the buttermilk, and return to the flour mix for a second coat.

6 Add 4 to 6 onion rings at a time to the hot oil, and fry 2 to 3 minutes on each side or until golden brown. Transfer the onion rings to a cooling rack.

7 After the onion rings are cooked, bread and fry the fish, double coating it with the flour mixture. Make sure the oil remains at 350°F (180°C), and fry the fish for 3 to 4 minutes on each side. Transfer to the cooling rack.

Tartar Sauce

1 In a small bowl, combine all of the ingredients. Stir well, and set aside.

Spicy Oil

1 In a medium bowl, combine all of the ingredients. To the bowl of spices, ladle 1 cup (250ml) of hot frying oil and stir.

2 Dip the fried fish into the chili oil, coating each filet generously. Place the oil-coated filets back on the cooling rack.

Assembly

1 To assemble, spread one side of each piece of bread with a generous amount of tartar sauce. Sandwich the fried fish and kelp pickles between two slices of bread.

2 Enjoy the spicy fish sandwich with onion rings and a side of tartar sauce for dipping.

For the onion rings and fried fish

- 1lb (450g) fish filet, cut into 2 pieces, each 4 x 4in (10 x 10cm)
- 4 tsp (24g) kosher salt
- 4 cups (1L) canola oil
- 2 cups (500ml) buttermilk (or 2 cups [500ml] whole milk combined with 1 tbsp [16ml] lemon juice)
- 2 tbsp (30ml) hot sauce
- 2 cups (240g) all-purpose flour
- ½ cup (65g) cornstarch
- ½ tbsp (4g) smoked paprika
- 1 tbsp (11g) onion powder
- 1 yellow onion, sliced and separated into ½-in (1.2cm) rings

For the tartar sauce

- ½ cup (125ml) Greek yogurt
- ¼ cup (60ml) mayo
- 2 tbsp (30g) chopped pickled onions
- ½ tbsp (8ml) lemon juice
- ½ tbsp (8ml) lime juice
- ¼ cup (30g) chopped kelp pickles or dill pickles
- 1 tbsp (6g) chopped cilantro stems

For the spicy oil

- 1 tsp (3g) onion powder
- 1 tsp (3g) garlic powder
- 1 tsp (3g) smoked paprika
- 1 tsp (3g) cayenne pepper
- 1 tsp (3g) black pepper
- 2 tsp (6g) chipotle chili powder
- 1 tbsp (12g) brown sugar

To assemble

- 4 slices grilled sourdough or 2 toasted brioche buns
- ½ cup (50g) kelp pickles or sliced dill pickles

Scan for bonus content.

Butterflied Rockfish with Tomato Gochujang Sauce

serves **2** | prep **10 minutes** | cook **15 minutes**

Rockfish is an extremely versatile white fish known for its firm but flaky, tender meat. It's best to cut the spine off using kitchen shears when fileting due to its sharp spine bones. A friend of mine was fishing for rockfish and got a spine in his hand—he ended up having to go to the ER and was diagnosed with what's known as "fish finger," which involves redness, swelling, and extreme pain.

This recipe uses butterflied, skin-on rockfish, but any fish filet with skin or no skin is suitable.

1 To a medium pan over medium heat, add 1 teaspoon cooking oil. Add the onion and sauté for 1 minute. Add the cherry tomatoes and garlic, and sauté for another 2 minutes. With a spatula or fork, lightly crush the cherry tomatoes. Add the white wine, fish sauce, gochujang, and miso paste. Bring to a simmer, then add the corn and thyme. Simmer for an additional 1 to 2 minutes. Remove from the heat, and set aside.

2 To make quick-pickled red onion, add the rice vinegar, ½ cup (125ml) water, and ½ teaspoon salt to a small saucepan. Bring to a simmer over medium heat, then add the sliced red onions. Simmer for 2 minutes, then remove from the heat and set aside.

3 In a large cast-iron skillet or similar, heat the remaining oil over medium-high heat. Lightly salt the fish on both sides. When the oil is hot or starts to smoke, add the fish, skin side down. Using a spatula, press the fish firmly onto the skillet for at least 10 seconds or until the fish no longer curls around the edges. Cook for 5 minutes on the skin side. If you notice the skin starting to burn, reduce the heat to medium. Flip the fish over and cook for an additional 4 minutes. Pull the fish off the skillet and let rest on a cooling rack.

4 Before serving, warm the sauce over medium-low heat for 2 minutes. Plate the sauce first, then place the fish over top. Finish with a layer of the quick-pickled red onion, and garnish with chives and flaky sea salt.

2 tbsp (30ml) cooking oil, divided

¼ yellow onion, finely diced

2 cups (450g) cherry tomatoes, whole

4 garlic cloves, chopped

½ cup (125ml) dry white wine

1 tsp (5ml) fish sauce

1 tbsp (15g) gochujang

½ tbsp (7g) white miso paste

¼ cup (36g) corn

Pinch of thyme

¼ cup (60ml) rice vinegar

½ tsp (3g) salt, plus more to taste

½ red onion, thinly sliced

2–3lb (1-1.4kg) rockfish, butterflied

1 tsp (1g) chopped chives, to garnish

½ tsp (3g) flaky sea salt, to garnish

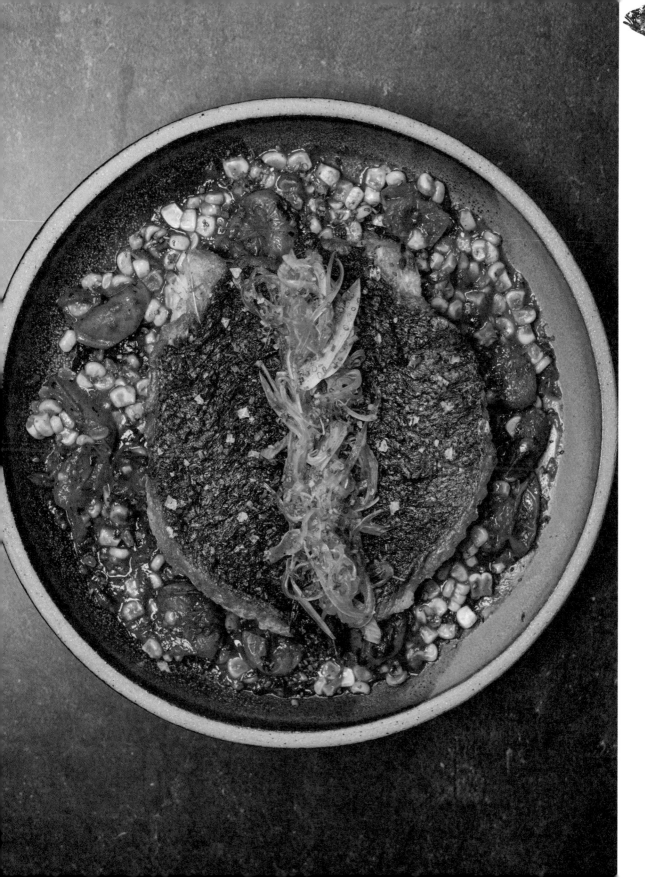

Bonito Tataki

makes **3–4 plates** | prep **20 minutes** | cook **1 minute**

The southern part of Japan specializes in making a dish out of what is considered to be "trash fish" in the US and other parts of the world. The fish is bled upon catching to preserve the freshness of the meat, then immediately placed on ice. This step is crucial for the best results. The fish is then fileted into quarters, aka gomai oroshi. Metal skewers are used to hold the filet above a fire to get a good sear on the skin. Traditionally, a handful of hay is used to create a quick burst of fire, but using a blowtorch to sear the skin will also work.

1 Using 3 to 5 metal skewers, pierce the filet to prop it up. Sprinkle the salt evenly on all sides of the filet. Place a handful of hay on an outdoor barbecue grill and light the hay on fire with a match or a lighter. As the hay burns, place the filet in the fire, skin-side down. Light more hay on fire 2 to 3 times as needed and check the skin for blistering. Once the skin is evenly blistered, transfer the filet to a cutting board and let it cool, skin-side down.

2 When cool, use a sharp knife to thinly slice the filet into sashimi pieces.

3 Plate the sashimi with a generous amount of ponzu, white onion, green onion, grated daikon radish, and grated ginger. Finish with a sprinkle of sesame seeds.

1lb (450g) skipjack or bonito filet

1 tbsp (18g) salt

2 tbsp (30ml) ponzu

¼ white onion, thinly sliced

1 bunch of green onions, sliced

2 tbsp (30g) grated daikon radish

1 tsp (5g) grated ginger

1 tsp (3g) sesame seeds

Whole Braised Fish over Crispy Noodles

serves **2** | prep **10 minutes** | cook **25 minutes**

The easiest way to utilize the whole fish without any waste is by cooking it whole. Rockfish, snapper, grouper, or any fish between 1 and 5 pounds (450g–2kg) is great for cooking whole. If you have a large pan, the fish should fit no problem, but the tail may need to be cut for it to fit into anything smaller. The fish will need to be scaled and gutted, as scales are unpleasant to eat when braised. Fish have a lot of meat in their heads and collars, which are often left out and tossed into the garbage. Braising is the perfect way to enjoy the whole fish with very little effort.

1   In a roasting pan or an enameled cast-iron pan, heat 1 tablespoon canola oil over medium-high heat. When hot, add the onion and julienned ginger. Season with the salt and pepper, and cook for 2 minutes. Add the green onions, carrot, bok choy, mirin, and vegetable stock, and bring to a simmer.

2   Once simmering, push the vegetables to one side of the pan, and add the fish. Cover with a lid and simmer on low heat for 16 to 20 minutes, or until the fish is fully cooked.

3   In a small bowl, mix the cornstarch with ½ cup (125ml) cold water to create a cornstarch slurry, then add it into the pan and bring to a boil over high heat. The braising liquid should thicken into a gravy-like consistency.

4   Heat a large wok or pan over medium-high heat. Add the rest of the canola oil and the fresh noodles, spreading the noodles out evenly. Fry for 2 to 4 minutes or until the noodles are crispy. Remove from the oil and drain on a cooling rack.

5   To a large family-size sharing plate, place the noodles on the bottom, and put the fish on top of the noodles. Pour the braising liquid along with all the vegetables over the top, and enjoy.

1 cup (250ml) canola oil, divided

1 onion, cubed

Two 2-in (5cm) pieces ginger, julienned

1 tsp (6g) salt

2 tsp (6g) black pepper

1 bunch of green onions, cut into 3-in (7.6cm) pieces

1 carrot, julienned

4 heads of bok choy, chopped

3 tbsp (45ml) mirin

3 cups (750ml) vegetable stock

1–3lb (0.5–1.4kg) whole fish, scored with 3 diagonal cuts on each side

1 tbsp (8g) cornstarch

10oz (300g) fresh noodles

Ceviche

serves **2–4** | prep **25 minutes** | cook **None**

Mexican ceviche is highly versatile and makes for a great meal. It's easy to make and can use just about any fish that's safe to eat raw. The lime cooks the fish with its acidity, but according to online sources, it does not kill parasites. For that reason, never use freshwater fish for ceviche. Use saltwater fish like halibut, snapper, sea bass, yellowtail, mahi mahi, grouper, rockfish, or tuna. The key ingredients are lime, cilantro, and onion. Feel free to mix it up, or try my version with wasabi and nori.

1   To the filet, sprinkle a generous amount of salt on all sides. Let sit on a plate for 10 to 15 minutes. Rinse off the salt, and pat dry with paper towels.

2   Using a sharp knife, slice the filet into ¼-inch (6mm) cubes. Add the cubed fish to a medium bowl along with the lime juice. Gently mix, and then let sit for 10 minutes.

3   After 10 minutes, add the rest of the ingredients to the bowl and mix. Serve on a tostada or enjoy with tortilla chips!

1lb (450g) fish filet
¼ cup (70g) salt
½ cup (125ml) lime juice
½ red onion, sliced
1–3 habanero or serrano peppers, chopped
1 bunch of cilantro, chopped
8–10 cherry tomatoes, quartered
½ English cucumber, cubed
1 avocado, cubed
1 tsp (2g) dried oregano
2 sheets of nori, crushed into fine bits
2 tsp (10g) wasabi

Baitfish: Herring, Anchovy, and Mackerel

Eating baitfish is underrated in Western cultures. There are multiple benefits to eating baitfish, starting with the sustainability factor. Wild-caught northern anchovies in the US are a smart choice for sustainable seafood according to the National Oceanic and Atmospheric Administration (NOAA). Anchovies, along with many more species, are responsibly harvested under strict US regulations. There are also better health benefits associated with baitfish than there are for most other fish. They are high in omega-3 fatty acids, vitamin A, calcium, and iron. Because baitfish are at the bottom of the food chain, they don't accumulate as much biotoxins and mercury as other seafood. They can be bought canned, fresh, and sometimes live and are the cheapest option for seafood. Although you can buy baitfish, there's nothing more sustainable than catching your own.

Catching baitfish is a lot of fun, and they are one of the easiest types of fish to catch. The best places to harvest baitfish are local piers and wharves during sunrise and sunset. All you need is a light rod and a Sabiki rig with a ½- to 1-ounce (14–28g) weight. A Sabiki rig is a line rigged with multiple small hooks that have a small piece of shiny material wrapped around them. You can tip the hooks with a small piece of squid or other bait, but it is not necessary.

The types of baitfish you catch will depend on your region. In Southern California, you'll likely catch mackerel and sardines. From Northern California to Alaska, you'll likely catch anchovies, smelt, and herring. In New Zealand, however, pilchard, jack mackerel, koheru, and piper are abundant. Wherever you are in the world, baitfish are a fun and delicious catch for the table.

There are many easy preparations with which to process baitfish. The bones of smaller fish like anchovies and sardines are delicate enough that you can eat the fish whole without a problem. In Japan, the easiest and most common way of preparing small fish like mackerel is to grill them over charcoal. Prepare the fish by scaling and gutting them as usual. Skewer and salt the fish generously, then cook over hot coals for 14 to 18 minutes. Check out the following recipes for more inspiration on ways to prepare and enjoy baitfish.

Shime Saba
(Vinegar-Cured Mackerel)

serves **2–4** | prep **20 minutes, plus 1 hour 25 minutes to cure** | cook **None**

Shime saba is a traditional Japanese technique for preparing mackerel that comes from a time when refrigeration was minimal. Yet the dish is still highly sought after by Japanese people today. The type of mackerel used is chub mackerel, usually about 8 to 12 inches (20–30cm) long with tiger stripes along its back. Similar fish like jack mackerel, opelu in Hawaii, or koheru in New Zealand would all work for this recipe. Mackerel has a high fat content and is often regarded by Westerners as "fishy," but there's nothing about mackerel to be scared of.

Mackerel can be easily caught from Monterey Bay down to Southern California. I grew up catching these fish off of public piers as a kid. It's one of the easiest fish to catch in Southern California in places like the Santa Monica Pier and Santa Barbara. All you need is a Sabiki rig and a small weight. Sabiki rigs can be purchased at any tackle shop. They use tiny hooks with a small piece of shiny material to attract fish—you don't even need any bait!

1 Spread generous layer of kosher salt on a baking sheet. Place the mackerel filets skin side down on the salt. Sprinkle another thick layer of salt on top of the filets, making sure to cover the entire surface. Place in the refrigerator for 1 hour to cure.

2 Meanwhile, prepare the chive-cilantro oil. In a blender, combine the chives, cilantro, oil, and pinch of fine salt. Blend until smooth, then transfer to a glass jar and refrigerate for at least 30 minutes. As the mixture cools, the oil will separate from the rest of the ingredients. Use a cheesecloth or coffee filter to strain the chive-cilantro oil into a clean jar (discard the solids). Set aside until ready to serve.

3 Remove the salt covered filets from the fridge. Rinse the filets with cold water to wash away the salt, and pat dry with paper towels. Place the filets in a shallow food storage container. Add the rice vinegar to the container, making sure the filets are entirely covered. Refrigerate for 25 minutes.

4 Remove the filets from the vinegar and pat dry. With a knife, remove the rib cage. With tweezers, remove the pin bones. Finally, with your fingers, peel the skin off as you would remove tape. Slice the filets into small bite-size pieces.

5 To serve, spoon some chive-cilantro oil onto a plate, then place the cured mackerel over top. Finish with a sprinkle of flaky sea salt and lime zest.

1 cup (225g) kosher salt
2–3 fresh mackerel, fileted with skin on
2 cups (500ml) rice vinegar
½ tsp (3g) flaky sea salt, to garnish
Zest of 1 lime, to garnish

For the chive-cilantro oil
¼ cup (12g) chopped chives
1 bunch of cilantro
½ cup (125ml) neutral oil
Pinch of fine salt

Herring Sando
with Horseradish Sauce

serves **4** | prep **25 minutes** | cook **15 minutes**

Herring is my favorite baitfish. In the San Francisco Bay Area, fishermen go wild for herring season, which is usually around January or February. (It's up to the fish!) They can be caught from piers, shore, or boats using a cast net. A Sabiki rig can be effective as well. Common places I have caught herring are Sausalito, Tiburon, Ferry Point Pier in Richmond, and Mission Bay in San Francisco. Many fishermen save these fish as bait for halibut, lingcod, and rockfish for the rest of the year as they are great at luring fish. Herring is meaty and can be just as good to eat.

If you want to save herring for bait, I suggest soaking them in a salt brine for 3 hours. Pat them dry and lay them on a baking sheet covered with parchment paper, ensuring the pieces don't touch. Freeze for 1 to 2 hours so they are half frozen and then vacuum pack and freeze the fish. Freezing them halfway first prevents the blood from getting pulled out of the fish when vacuum sealing, making for a much cleaner job. You will ultimately end up with a higher-quality bait, increasing your chances of catching more fish.

1   To make the herring, prepare a dredging station. Crack the eggs into a shallow bowl and lightly beat them. In a second shallow bowl, combine the panko breadcrumbs and furikake. Add the flour to a third shallow bowl.

2   Take one herring and dredge both sides with flour, shaking off the excess. Next, dip in the beaten eggs. Lastly, coat with the panko mix. Repeat for each herring.

3   In a large cast-iron skillet, heat the canola oil over medium heat. When it starts to smoke, add 2 herrings, one at a time. Fry both sides for 3 to 4 minutes each. Once both sides of the herring are golden brown, remove from the skillet and set aside on a wire rack to cool. Repeat with the remaining herrings.

4   To make the horseradish sauce, in a medium bowl, combine all of the ingredients and mix well.

5   To assemble the sandwiches, spread the sauce on one side of each piece of bread. On each of 4 slices of bread, place 1 herring and 1 poached egg. Close the sandwich placing the remaining slices of bread top of the poached eggs.

6   Cut the sandwiches in half diagonally, and serve.

For the herring

3 eggs

2 cups (120g) panko breadcrumbs

¼ cup (30g) furikake

½ cup (60g) all-purpose flour

8 herrings, butterflied and deboned

4 cups (1L) canola or frying oil

For the sauce

1 cup (250g) plain Greek yogurt

½ cup (40g) grated horseradish

½ tbsp (8ml) lemon juice

¼ cup (35g) chopped fresh dill

¼ cup (25g) chopped green onion

1 tsp (6g) sea salt

1 tsp (3g) black pepper

To assemble

8 slices white bread

4 poached eggs

Sweet and Sour Anchovies

serves **3–4** | prep **20 minutes** | cook **15 minutes**

Fresh anchovies can be caught in the open ocean on the West Coast of the US. In the Bay Area, you can catch them most often in the summer months. Use Sabiki rigs with the smallest hooks. If you can't catch them on your own, you can buy live anchovies in San Francisco at J&P Bait. Check their Facebook page for updates on availability. Most people use the fresh anchovies for bait to catch halibut or striped bass, but they are completely fine to eat!

Many fishermen tend to have a rule on not eating bait, but that's just irrational. Baitfish like anchovies have the least amount of contaminants, as they are at the bottom of the food chain. They are also rich in omega-3s and a sustainable source of seafood. Anchovies are small and have soft bones, so there's no need to filet them. Simply take the head off and eat them whole. This recipe, inspired by traditional Chinese sweet and sour pork, works great with these little baitfish.

1 Begin by cleaning the anchovies. With a small knife, cut off the head and make an incision down the belly. Using your finger, remove the guts and blood line. Rinse under cold water.

2 In a large bowl, combine prepare a mixture of water and salt (roughly 3 percent of the weight of the anchovies). Soak the anchovies in the salt water for 15 minutes, then remove and pat dry.

3 Meanwhile, make the sauce. In a small bowl, combine all of the sauce ingredients and mix well. Set aside until ready to use.

4 In a medium bowl, combine flour and pepper. Add the soy sauce and cleaned anchovies, and toss to coat. If the flour is too thick, add 1 tablespoon (15ml) water and mix again.

5 In a large wok or pan heat the oil over medium-high heat to 350°F (180°C). While the oil is heating, to a medium bowl, add the cornstarch. Dip one anchovy into the cornstarch so it's evenly coated. To test that the oil is hot enough, place the prepared anchovy into the hot oil. If it starts to sizzle immediately, the oil is hot enough. Coat the anchovies in cornstarch one at a time, then place 6 to 8 anchovies into the hot oil. Cook for 4 minutes or until golden brown. Remove and set aside on a cooling rack to drain the oil. Repeat with the remaining anchovies.

6 With a paper towel, clean out the same wok or pan, then place over high heat and add the sauce. Allow the sauce to reduce for 3 to 5 minutes, stirring occasionally.

7 Once the sauce thickens, add the onion and bell pepper, and cook for 1 to 2 minutes. Add the anchovies, and mix it all together. Plate on a large dish, and enjoy with a side of fried rice or chow mein.

For the anchovies
1lb (450g) fresh anchovies
1 tbsp (8g) all-purpose flour
1 tsp (3g) black pepper
2 tbsp (30ml) soy sauce
1 cup (250ml) canola oil
½ cup (60g) cornstarch
½ red onion, cubed
1 bell pepper (red, yellow, or green), cubed

For the sauce
3 tbsp (45ml) ketchup
2 tbsp (30ml) brown sugar
1 tsp (3g) cornstarch
½ tsp (3g) salt
2 tbsp (30ml) rice vinegar

Scan for bonus content.

"Eat It All" Fish Head, Guts, and Skin

There is so much more to fish than the filets, just as there is more to a chicken than the breast. You can eat just about every part of a fish, from the head to the tail, and it has the potential to be much tastier, juicier, and more texturally unique if prepared well. One aspect of sustainability I'm passionate about is reducing food waste. Using the entire fish not only shows respect toward its life but also gives you more to work with. Parts that are often thrown out, like the fish head, bones, and the contents of the gut cavity, can open up a whole new world of potential culinary creativity.

Different parts of the fish lend themselves to various cooking methods and dishes. For instance, the head and collar are prized in some cultures for their tender meat and unique flavors. The bones can be roasted and used to enhance the umami profile of dishes, while the skin can be crisped up for a delightful texture. Within the gut cavity, there is the liver, stomach, and sometimes eggs, which in most fish are all edible. Fish liver is very similar in flavor and texture to chicken liver. Fish stomach has a slight chewy and crunchy texture that is great fried or grilled; it can even be simmered to make it soft and tender. For the best yield, harvest these parts from fish bigger than 20 inches (50cm). Reducing food waste is ethical and also has environmental benefits. By making the most of every part of the fish, we contribute to sustainability efforts by decreasing the overall demand for seafood and the resources needed to catch and process it.

I love all the different parts of fish because of their unique textures. It's comparable to a yakitori chef breaking down chicken. According to YouTube's popular yakitori specialist, Yakitoriguy, there are easily over twenty different cuts from a single chicken that can be made into yakitori. All the different parts like the gizzard, skin, cartilage, and more, are utilized in yakitori. If we can get our minds to think about fish in a similar manner, more parts of the fish would be prized. In the US, the most prized piece of fish is a boneless and skinless filet, which is, in my opinion, the most boring piece of fish. It's basically the chicken breast of fish: mild, bland, and easily overcooked. In this section, I share a variety of recipes that star the underutilized parts of a fish. There is a method that makes the skin puffy, airy, and crunchy. It requires a little extra effort beyond just frying it, but it's entirely worth it. I also share a recipe using fish head in a unique way, one on how to cook fish stomach, and yet another on how to use the bones to make the best miso soup. If you're feeling adventurous, these delicious recipes will surely make you excited to try more unique fish parts.

Tuna Menudo

serves **4** | prep **30 minutes** | cook **4 hours 15 minutes**

Menudo is one of my favorite Mexican dishes. It uses cow stomach, also known as tripe, which is simmered for a long time in soup, allowing it to become tender and delicious. It's one of those miracle hangover foods.

I decided to experiment using fish stomach, and the results were amazing. I first used the head and bones to make a stock with a uniquely deep flavor that's a lot lighter than beef stock. After simmering the tuna stomach, the consistency was tender yet meaty. I've only tried it with bluefin tuna, but I imagine it would work well with other big or pelagic fish.

Pro tip: If you're ever on a charter boat, ask for the pieces they throw overboard to make your stock. That's exactly what I did when I went on a tuna charter out of San Diego, California!

For the stock
5lb (2.25kg) fish heads and carcass

For the stomach
1lb (450g) tuna stomach (or other pelagic fish)

For the salsa
8 guajillo peppers, seeds and stems removed
¼ large yellow onion
3 garlic cloves
1 sprig of epazote (optional)

To finish
½ large yellow onion
1 tbsp (15g) kosher salt
1 cup (250g) canned hominy

To serve
2 limes, sliced
¼ large yellow onion, chopped
½ bunch of cilantro, chopped
1 tsp (2g) red pepper flakes
1 tsp (2g) dried oregano
Salt to taste

Stock

1 Fill a large stock pot three-fourths full with water and bring to a boil.

2 Add the heads and carcass, and simmer for 2 hours. Scoop out scum and impurities every 5 to 20 minutes as it simmers, more frequently in the beginning.

3 Strain the bones out of the stock to finish and let cool until the fat solidifies at the top. Run a clean paper towel over the surface to remove the fat, then discard the paper towel. Set the stock aside.

Stomach

1 Clean the fish stomach by butterflying it open and rinsing under cold water.

2 In a small pot, bring water to a boil. Add the stomach and simmer for 5 minutes. Strain and rinse under cold water.

3 Cut the stomach into 1 x 1-inch (2.5 x 2.5cm) portions. Set aside.

Salsa

1 In a medium pan over medium heat, lightly toast the guajillo peppers for 5 minutes. Turn frequently to avoid burning.

2 Add 2 cups (500ml) water to the pan and simmer for 8 to 10 minutes, then let cool.

3 In a blender, combine the guajillo peppers, simmering liquid, onion, garlic cloves, and epazote, if using. Blend until it creates a smooth salsa consistency, then strain the salsa through a sieve.

Finish

1 Bring the fish stock back to a boil and add the onion. Add the salsa, prepared fish stomach, and salt. Simmer for 2 to 4 hours, depending on how you like the texture.

2 In the last 10 minutes of simmering, add the hominy.

Serve

1 Serve in a bowl with a slice of lime, chopped onions, cilantro, chili, and oregano. Add salt to taste.

Note
Epazote can be hard to come by, so you will need to visit a specialty Mexican market for this ingredient. Guajillo peppers and canned hominy are usually available at your typical big-name supermarkets.

Birria Fish Head Tacos

serves **4** | prep **20 minutes** | cook **2 hours**

People tend to throw away fish heads, but if you learn how easy it is to make a delicious meal with them, you'll never waste them again! The head contains a lot of meat that is more unique in texture than the average filet. The cheeks are scallop-like, and the tops of the heads are like chicken tenders. All the meat can be easily removed by boiling. This is another Mexican-inspired recipe that's sure to get people excited for fish heads.

You can make this recipe with any fish of your choice. The amount of meat you get from the fish heads will depend on the size of fish you use. The head of a 20-pound (9kg) yellowtail will yield roughly 2 cups of meat. If the collar is included, it will yield up to 4 cups of meat, which is enough to feed 3 to 4 people. In contrast, the head and collar of a 2- to 4-pound (1-1.8kg) rockfish will yield about ½ cup of meat. Either way, that's a lot of meat you'll miss out on if you throw it away!

1 Preheat the oven or grill to 450°F (230°C).

2 Place the whole fish heads over a fire, on a grill, or in the oven for 4 minutes or until lightly charred. At the same time, char the tomatoes, guajillo and arbol peppers, and the onion. Set the charred vegetables aside.

3 In a stock pot, bring 8 cups (2L) water to a boil over high heat. Add the fish heads, and reduce the heat to low. Simmer for 25 to 30 minutes, depending on the size of the fish heads. Take out the fish heads, and remove all the meat from the heads and bones. Shred the meat, and set aside.

4 Strain the stock into a large bowl to get rid of any bones, then pour the stock back into the stock pot. Discard the bones.

5 To a blender, add the charred tomatoes, guajillo and arbol peppers, and the onion, along with the garlic and oregano. Add 1½ cups (375ml) of the fish head stock and blend together to make a sauce.

6 In a medium saucepan, heat the canola oil over medium heat for 3 minutes. Add the blended sauce to the hot oil and bring to a simmer. Stir in the reserved meat from the fish heads. Taste and season with salt if needed, then add 4 cups (1L) of the remaining fish head stock.

7 Using a slotted spoon, scoop the fish head meat from the pot, leaving behind the consommé. Turn off the heat. As the consommé cools, a layer of oil will form on the surface. Using a large spoon or ladle, skim off the oil and collect it in a shallow bowl. Set aside.

8 Preheat a flat-top grill or nonstick skillet over medium-high heat.

9 Dip a tortilla into the reserved oil, coating both sides. Immediately place it on the hot flat-top grill and cook for 1 minute. Flip the tortilla, and to one half of opposite side, add some fish head meat, minced onion, and queso Oaxaca. Fold the tortilla over to make a taco, and cook for 2 minutes on both sides. Repeat using the remaining tortillas, meat, onion, and queso Oaxaca.

10 Serve immediately, topped with minced onion, cilantro, queso cotija, and a squeeze of lime, as well as a side of consommé for dipping.

2 or more fish heads (enough to yield 3–4 cups of meat)
2 Roma tomatoes
8 dried guajillo peppers
3 dried chile de arbol peppers
1 white onion, halved
8 garlic cloves
1 tsp (2g) dried oregano
¾ cup (175ml) canola oil
Twelve 6-in (15cm) corn tortillas
½ white onion, minced
One 10oz (283g) package queso or shredded mozzarella

To serve
Minced white onion
Chopped fresh cilantro
Crumbled queso cotija or queso fresco
Lime wedges

Scan for bonus content.

Fish Skin Crackling with Uni

makes **7 ounces (200g)** | prep **10 minutes** | cook **5 minutes**

Fish skin is another part of the fish that is underutilized. Most fishermen tend to leave the scales on while fileting, and in most dishes, scales are inedible, hence the reason people get rid of the whole skin. Scaling fish has multiple benefits, and being able to eat the skin is one of them. Keeping the skin on for the cooking process also keeps the filet juicy and protects it from easily overcooking.

If you're a fan of chicharrones, aka pork cracklings, you have to try this crispy fish skin recipe. It's light, airy, crispy, and not as fishy as you might expect. It's only right that I give credit to Hank Shaw for the inspiration of this recipe. He did it with sturgeon skin, which is tough, so it can be done with practically any fish. This method is ten times better than just frying. You'll need to first boil the skin, then dehydrate it using either a dehydrator or an oven set to the lowest setting.

1 Fill a medium pot halfway with water, and bring to a boil over high heat. Add the skin and boil for 3 minutes.

2 Remove the skin from the water, and spread evenly in a single layer on the tray of a dehydrator. Dehydrate at 100°F (38°C) for 6 to 8 hours or until the skin has hardened. Once dried, allow it to cool.

3 In a deep saucepan, heat the oil to 300°F (150°C). Fry the skin for 5 to 10 seconds until it starts to puff. Once it stops puffing up, remove from the oil and set on a wire rack to cool.

4 Top the fish crackling with uni and ikura, and garnish with chives.

Fish skin from 1 salmon filet, scaled
1 cup (250ml) canola oil
3½ oz (100g) uni (sea urchin)
2oz (55g) ikura or caviar
Minced chives, to garnish

Note
If you're not using the dehydrated fish skin immediately, you can store it in a sealed jar for up to a week before frying.

Mentaiko (Spicy Fish Roe)

makes **1 pound (450g)** | prep **10 minutes** | cook **2 minutes**

Most fishermen throw out any and all guts inside a fish, but even if you choose not to consume the liver or stomach, you should always keep the roe (fish eggs). For this recipe, use a fish roe that has small, fine, individual eggs, like cod, sea bass, or snapper. The skein, or membrane, of the roe can contain parasites, so freeze the roe sack before preparing this recipe. See page 34 for freezing instructions.

This recipe is inspired by the Japanese mentaiko, which uses roe from pollock, a member of the cod family. It's often used as a condiment for rice and even pasta. It's a mildly spicy and savory dish with a unique texture.

1 On a baking sheet, sprinkle a heavy layer of salt and lay the roe sack on top. Cover the top with more salt. Leave in a cool environment for 8 to 12 hours to cure.

2 Once cured, rinse off all the salt. Using a paper towel, pat dry. Set aside.

3 In a medium saucepan, combine the sake and mirin. Bring to a simmer over medium heat. Once simmering, light with a torch or lighter to burn off the alcohol. You can also tilt the saucepan to catch fire if you're using a gas burner.

4 Add the soy sauce, gochujang, and chili powder to the sake-mirin mixture. Stir the marinade thoroughly, then turn off the heat and let cool to room temperature.

5 To a medium container, add the roe and marinade. To ensure full submersion, place a paper towel over the roe.

6 Allow the roe to marinate for 24 to 48 hours, depending on the size of the roe.

7 Once marinated, remove the roe and let it dry off. It is now ready for use.

2 cups (450g) kosher salt
1lb (450g) sack of roe
½ cup (125ml) sake
½ cup (125ml) mirin
¼ cup (60ml) soy sauce
½ cup (125ml) gochujang
1 tbsp (6g) chili powder or gochugaru

Note
Use this mentaiko to create the mentaiko pasta on the next page.

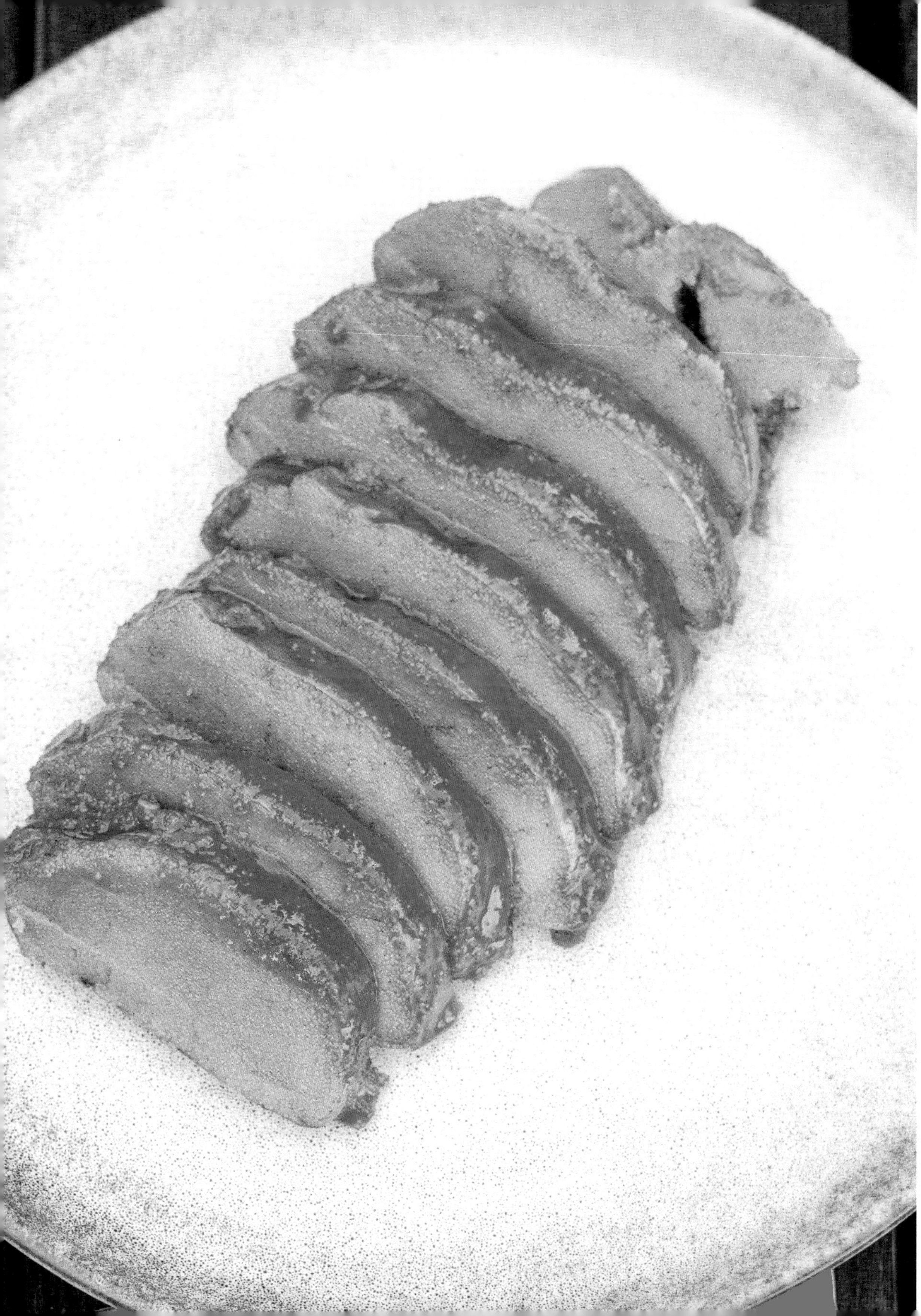

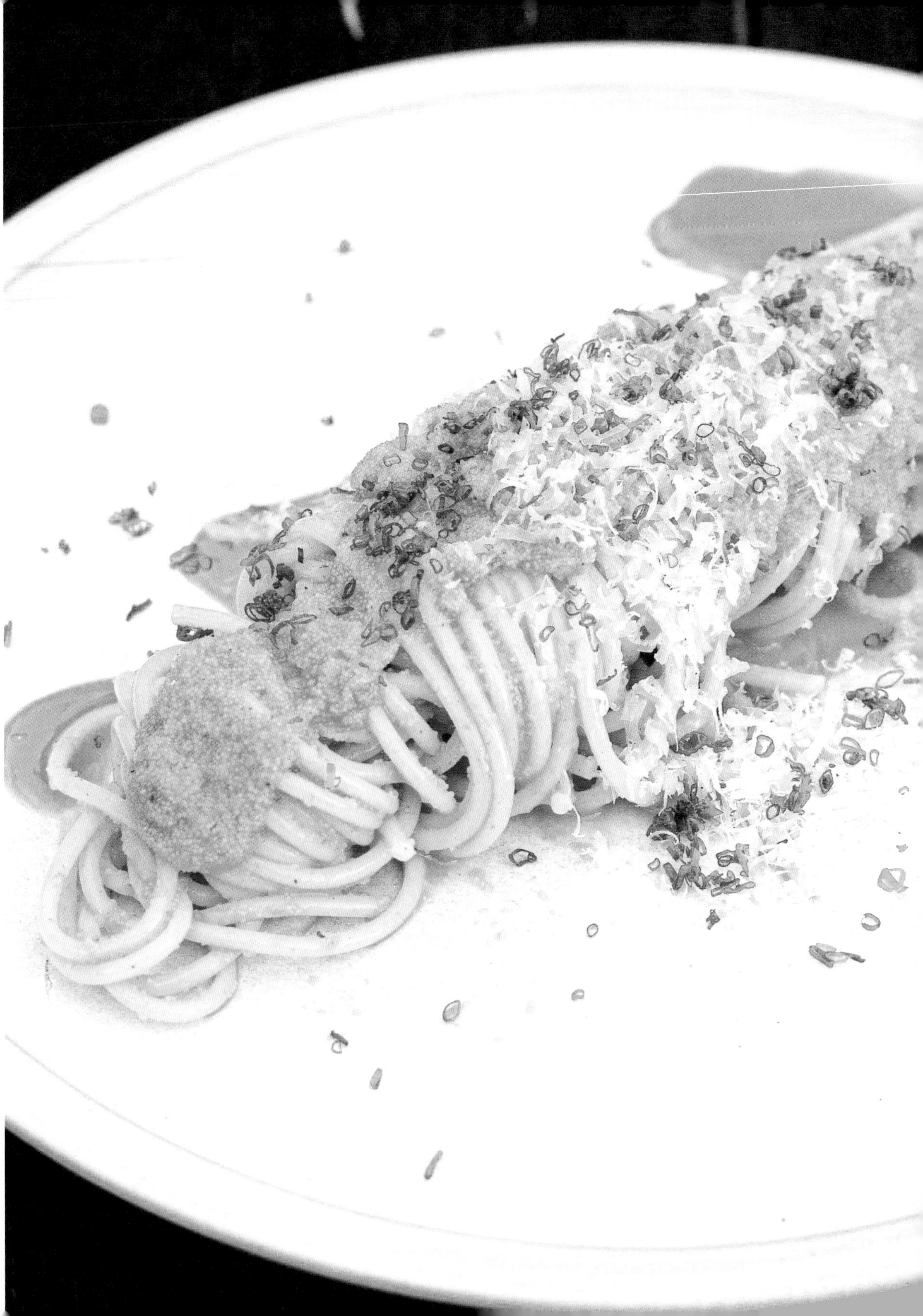

Mentaiko Pasta

serves **4** | prep **10 minutes** | cook **15 minutes**

One way to utilize the mentaiko recipe (see page 140) is to make mentaiko pasta, a popular spaghetti recipe in Japan. You can also buy premade fresh mentaiko at Japanese markets, which can be expensive, or you can get mentaiko spaghetti seasoning in the dry-foods section of your supermarket to make this dish—it's much cheaper than buying fresh mentaiko. The roe provides a briny, salty, and spicy flavor and slightly granular texture that give this dish a uniqueness of its own. Combined with al dente spaghetti, it really is a perfect bite.

1 Fill a large pot three-fourths full with water and bring to a boil over high heat. Once boiling, season generously with salt and add the spaghetti. Cook according to package instructions or until al dente.

2 Meanwhile, in a medium bowl, combine the mentaiko, eggs, and Parmesan. Mix thoroughly to combine. Set aside.

3 Drain the spaghetti in a colander, reserving ¼ cup (60ml) of the pasta water.

4 In a saucepan or deep skillet over medium-high heat, sear the guanciale for 2 minutes. Once seared, add the cooked spaghetti and reserved pasta water to the pan. Turn off the heat.

5 Add the mentaiko sauce and mix. The residual heat of the pan will cook the sauce into the spaghetti.

6 Serve immediately, garnished with Parmesan, chives, and lemon zest, if using.

Salt, to taste

10oz (300g) spaghetti

8oz (225g) mentaiko, membrane scraped off

2 eggs

½ cup (225g) grated Parmesan cheese, plus more to garnish

6oz (175g) guanciale or pancetta, diced

Minced chives, to garnish

Zest of 1 lemon (optional), to garnish

Scan for bonus content.

Fish Bone Miso Soup

serves **8–10** | prep **5 minutes** | cook **3 hours**

One of the easiest ways to use fish bones and scraps is to make a broth. In the restaurants I worked at, I used fish bones to make miso soup every day. A really simple way is to boil the bones, combine the broth with dashi, and then mix with miso. This recipe will go one step further to create a delicious miso soup, incorporating the techniques restaurants use to get the best results. Many white fish, like flounder, snapper, rockfish, grouper, etc., can be used for creating a nice, clean-flavored broth. The most important thing is to clean the fish heads of any gills and blood and rinse under cold water.

1 In a large pot, bring 6⅓ cups (1.5L) of water to boil in a large pot over high heat. Add the fish bones and scraps, and simmer over low heat for 1 hour. Strain the bones and impurities out, and let the broth cool until the fat rises to the surface. Discard the used fish bones.

2 Once the fat has risen to the top of the stock, gently place paper towels on the surface and drag across to remove the fat. Repeat 2 to 3 times.

3 Add the dashi to the stock. Next, add the miso paste by dipping a sieve halfway into the stock, dropping the miso into the sieve, and using a whisk to incorporate the miso paste. The sieve will help break up the miso as well as catch any little bits of soybean.

4 Remove the sieve, discarding any accumulated bits of soybean. Before serving, bring the soup to a simmer over medium heat. Serve hot.

2–4lb (1–1.8kg) fish bones and scraps, cleaned and patted dry
4¼ cups (1L) dashi
2½ tbsp (38ml) miso paste

Note
Use this base for ramen and other soups, or add the picked meat, dried seaweed, and enoki mushroom for a nice miso soup.

Fish Liver Pâté

makes **12 ounces (340g)** | prep **15 minutes, plus overnight to cool** | cook **25 minutes**

Fish liver is an underutilized part of the fish. Halibut, lingcod, and many others have large livers that can be put to good use. Fish liver tastes much like chicken liver, and it can be used in similar ways. Depending on the preparation, it can be soft, creamy, or buttery. If you're a fan of liver or pâté, you're going to love this recipe.

1 With a pair of tweezers, remove the large blood vessels from the fish liver. Evenly coat the liver with a light sprinkle of salt on both sides. Place in the refrigerator to cure for 10 minutes. Then rinse off the salt with cold water and pat dry with a paper towel.

2 Add the olive oil to a small saucepan and heat over medium heat. Add the onion, garlic, thyme, and bay leaf, and sauté for 3 to 4 minutes.

3 Add the dashi and soy sauce. Bring to a simmer, then add the fish liver. Simmer for 10 minutes.

4 Allow the saucepan to cool for at least 10 minutes. Remove the bay leaf, and add the rest of the mixture to a blender, including the broth. Add the butter, and blend for 1 to 2 minutes or until smooth. Transfer the mixture into a glass jar with a lid, and refrigerate overnight.

5 Enjoy pâté on toast or on Vietnamese sandwiches.

½lb (225g) fish liver
½ tbsp (9g) salt
2 tsp (10ml) olive oil
¼ white onion, sliced
3 garlic cloves, lightly crushed
Pinch of fresh thyme
1 bay leaf
½ cup (125ml) dashi or chicken stock
1 tsp (5ml) light soy sauce
4 tbsp (60g) butter, softened

Scan for bonus content.

SHELLFISH

Clams

Clams can be harvested in a variety of tidal environments like beaches, rocky intertidal zones, and mudflats. Different environments are home to different species. The large mudflats on the West Coast like Bodega Bay, Half Moon Bay, Coos Bay, and many more have horseneck clams and butter clams. Along the rocky intertidal areas of the same bays, you can find steamer clams. Some beaches from Northern California to Washington have razor clams. Harvesting clams is always a bit of work, but it is a lot of fun and definitely worth the trouble.

Before shucking freshly harvested clams, let the clams soak in ocean water (or salt water) for a minimum of 3 hours or up to 8 hours. It is important the water used for this step comes from a clean water source. If one isn't available, simply mix salt in filtered water to make a 3.5 percent salt brine. For example, mix 2 tablespoons (33g) salt for every 4¼ cups (1L) water. This will be the equivalent salinity to ocean water.

To store clams for longer than 8 hours, remove them from the salt water. Dampen two paper towels with salt water. Place one paper towel on the bottom of a container, add the clams, then place the other paper towel over top. Keep refrigerated for up to 2 days.

Shucking clams is easier than shucking oysters. There are two ways to go about this. The first way is to use a paring knife or pocketknife. Place the sharp side of the knife between the clamshells. Hold the clam and blade in each hand and push the backside of the knife into the shell using the fingers holding the blade. The knife will slide between the shells. Pull the shells apart to access the meat.

The second shucking method is to use a butter knife. Wedge the butter knife in the back of the clam (the hinge side). Turn the butter knife like a key to split the clam open. Use your fingers to pull off one side of the shell, leaving the meat in the other.

Scan for bonus content.

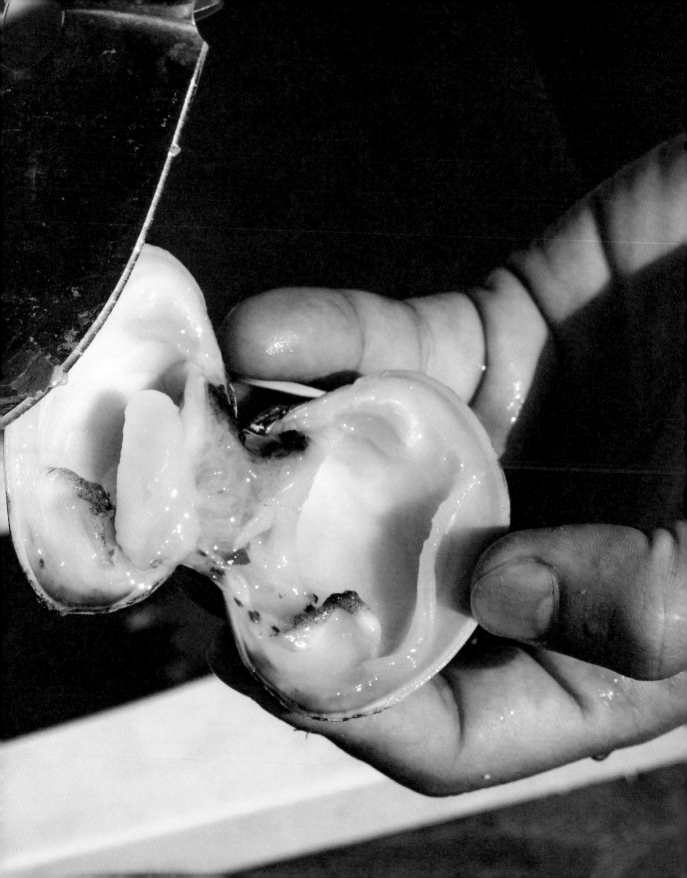

Raw Clams Three Ways

serves **2–4** | prep **15 minutes** | cook **None**

Like oysters, clams can be eaten raw. (In my opinion, clams on the half shell are even better than oysters.) The best types to eat raw are gaper clams, like geoducks and horse clams, which are quite large and not very common in markets. However, the more common steamer clams, like manilas and cockles, are also delicious raw. My favorite way to enjoy raw clams is simply with a small squeeze of lemon juice, but if you want to jazz them up, here are a few easy and quick topping options.

Option One: Shallot and Serrano

1 In a small bowl, combine the shallots, serrano pepper, vinegar, and 1 tablespoon (15ml) water. Mix well.

2 Arrange the half-shelled clams on a plate. Spoon the sauce over top of the clams, then garnish with lemon zest.

Option Two: Wasabi and Ponzu

1 In a small bowl, combine the shallots, wasabi, and ponzu. Mix well.

2 Arrange the half-shelled clams on a plate. Spoon the sauce over the clams. Top with a sprinkle of chives.

Option Three: Pickled Red Onion and Lime

1 Arrange the half-shelled clams on a plate. Top each clam with 1 piece of pickled red onion and a small pinch of ginger. Squeeze lime juice over each clam and top with lime zest.

For Option One
½ shallot, finely chopped
1 serrano pepper, finely chopped
1 tbsp (15ml) sherry vinegar
8oz (225g) steamer clams, shucked in half shells
Zest of 1 lemon, to garnish

For Option Two
½ tbsp (5g) finely chopped shallot
1 tsp (5g) wasabi paste
2 tbsp (30ml) ponzu
8oz (225g) steamer clams, shucked in half shells
1 tsp (1g) chopped chives

For Option Three
8oz (225g) steamer clams, shucked in half shells
¼ cup (20g) pickled red onion
1 tsp (5g) finely chopped fresh ginger
Juice of ½ lime
Zest of 1 lime

Scan for bonus content.

Garlic Butter Shrimp

serves **4** | prep **5 minutes** | cook **10 minutes**

This is my rendition of Hawaii's garlic butter shrimp. If you're ever driving along the North Shore of Oahu, make sure to stop by the food trucks selling garlic butter shrimp.

All over Hawaii, there are freshwater streams filled with freshwater prawns called Tahitian prawns, which are an invasive species in Hawaii that compete with and prey on native species. They look like regular prawns except they have long, thin claws. You can catch them in crawfish traps, or you can go in for a dive and spear them with a three-prong pole spear.

To devein the shrimp, slice the top side of the tail lengthwise and cut through the shell to access and remove the vein. Then rinse under cold water. The shrimp should be cooked fast over medium-high heat, which will make the shell nice and crunchy.

1 Place the shrimp in a large bowl. Add the cornstarch, and toss lightly to coat. Shake each shrimp to remove excess cornstarch and set aside.

2 In a large wok or frying pan, heat the cooking oil over high heat. When it starts to smoke, begin tossing in the shrimp one at a time, with up to 5 shrimp in the wok at once. Cook for 2 minutes on one side, then flip and cook the other side for another 1 to 2 minutes. Remove the shrimp from the wok and place on a cooling rack. Set aside.

3 With a paper towel, wipe out the wok or pan used to cook the shrimp. Heat the wok over medium heat. Add the butter. When the butter is almost completely melted, add the garlic, ginger, and jalapeño. Cook for 1 minute.

4 Add the soy sauce, honey, salt, and pepper to the wok, and mix it all together. Add the fried shrimp, and toss to evenly coat the shrimp in sauce. Turn off the heat.

5 Serve hot, garnished with green onion and a lemon wedge, if using.

1½–2lb (675–900g) shrimp, deveined, heads and shells on

1 cup (130g) cornstarch

½ cup (125ml) cooking oil, such as canola oil

6 tbsp (85g) unsalted butter

1 garlic head or 10 garlic cloves, chopped

2-in (5cm) piece ginger, julienned

1 jalapeño, sliced

1 tbsp (15ml) soy sauce

1 tbsp (15ml) honey

1 tsp (6g) salt

1 tsp (3g) black pepper

½ bunch of green onion, sliced, to garnish

4 lemon wedges (optional), to garnish

Note

The cornstarch helps the shrimp absorb the sauce. In step 2, do not add all the shrimp at once or it will drop the temperature of the cooking oil.

Scan for bonus content.

Gochujang Curry Mussels

serves **4** | prep **10 minutes** | cook **20 minutes**

To get the most flavor out of mussels, cook them in a sauce. This makes them release their strong, delicious seafood flavor, giving the sauce a deep flavor profile. This gochujang curry mussels recipe combines spice with nutty coconut and briny mussels. Out of all the mussel recipes I've tried, it is by far my favorite.

1 Prepare the green onions by chopping the bottom white parts into 1-inch (2.5cm) pieces. Thinly slice the green parts and set aside.

2 In a large saucepan or wok, heat the oil over medium heat, turning the pan to coat the cooking surface with oil.

3 To the preheated saucepan or wok, add the white parts of the green onion and the chopped yellow onion. Sauté for 30 seconds.

4 Add the garlic cloves, gochujang, and soy sauce. Toss everything together, then add the coconut milk and bring to a boil.

5 Once boiling, add the mussels. Cover with a lid, and boil for 6 minutes or until the mussels open.

6 Place the mussels in a large bowl, and top with sliced green onions and shredded coconut. Serve with a side of rice, if desired.

1 bunch of green onions
2 tsp (10ml) cooking oil
½ yellow onion, chopped
6 garlic cloves
2 tbsp (30ml) gochujang
½ tbsp (8ml) soy sauce
1 can (400ml) coconut milk
4lb (1.8kg) live mussels, cleaned
¼ cup (25g) shredded coconut
Cooked white rice (optional), to serve

Note

Be careful not to overcook the mussels. When 80 percent of the mussels have opened, they are done cooking. Mussels have a stronger adductor muscle than clams, making them harder to pop open. Often, not all of them will fully open, but they are completely safe to eat so long as they crack open a little bit.

Scan for bonus content.

Spiny Lobster Crudo

serves **2** | prep **15 minutes** | cook **None**

In the Pacific Ocean, we have what is known as spiny lobster, aka crayfish in Australia and New Zealand. The season for catching these delicious and highly prized lobsters usually runs from early October to mid-March. All you need are freediving gear and a pair of thick gloves. Spiny lobsters are often caught in shallow waters from 5 to 30 feet (1.5–9m) deep. The best time is at night when they come out of their rocks to look for food.

My favorite preparation for this seafood is raw. I have never seen a parasite in the meat of a spiny lobster and have never had an issue preparing them this way. One key ingredient that pairs well with this lobster is freshly grated Parmesan cheese. The age-old idea of cheese and seafood not pairing well should be thrown in the trash. With the different flavors and textures both seafood and cheese have to offer, there is undoubtedly a perfect match among them.

1 The shell of a spiny lobster is incredibly hard, which makes it difficult to dispatch from the top. Instead, I like to flip it on its back and insert a knife through the underside. The lobster should then go limp.

2 With a small knife, cut the membrane that attaches the head to the tail. Once you cut all the way around, twist the tail back and forth and pull apart to remove the tail. The tail contains most of the meat. Save the head for stock, or boil it to get the meat out of the antennae and legs.

3 Using kitchen shears, make two cuts along the underside of the tail, just inside the sharp spines. Peel the flap, then use a spoon to scoop out all the tail meat.

4 Slice the tail meat in half, lengthwise, and remove the vein. The tail meat is now ready to eat.

5 Cut the meat into bite-size pieces, and arrange them on a large plate, 1 inch (2.5cm) apart from one another.

6 Drizzle a generous amount of olive oil over the lobster, and top with the shallot, Parmesan, sea salt, and chives. Garnish with radish and lemon.

1 live spiny lobster
1 tbsp (15ml) olive oil
¼ shallot, thinly sliced
1 tbsp (8g) freshly grated Parmesan cheese
½ tsp (3g) flaky sea salt
1 tbsp (5g) minced chives
Sliced radish, to garnish
Lemon slices, to garnish

Scan for bonus content.

Yuzu Crab Cakes

serves **6–8** | prep **10 minutes** | cook **10 minutes**

I don't make crab cakes very often, but when I do, they're f****** good! This recipe incorporates Japanese flavors with a Western-style dish. Come to think of it, a lot of my dishes are exactly that. It makes sense because I'm Japanese American. All these recipes are literally me on a plate!

A good crab cake has a lot of crab and a little of everything else. This combination of yuzu and miso pairs perfectly with any kind of crab.

1 In a medium bowl, combine 1 cup (60g) panko, the egg, lemon zest, yuzu juice, green onions, miso, hondashi, mayo, and crab meat. Mix together well.

2 Using your hands, form six to eight 2-inch (5cm) cakes, and coat each with the remaining 3 cups (180g) panko.

3 In a large pan, heat the oil over medium heat. When hot, shallow fry the crab cakes for 3 to 4 minutes on each side or until golden brown.

4 Garnish with nori and katsuobushi sprinkled over top, if using.

4 cups (240g) panko breadcrumbs, divided

1 egg

Zest of 1 lemon

1 tbsp (15ml) yuzu juice (Japanese citrus) or lemon juice

¼ cup (25g) chopped green onions

2 tbsp (30ml) Saikyo miso or white miso

1 tsp (5ml) hondashi

2 tbsp (30ml) Kewpie mayo

1lb (450g) crab meat

2 tbsp (30ml) frying oil

Nori flakes (optional), to garnish

Katsuobushi (bonito flakes; optional), to garnish

Ganjang Gejang
(Korean Marinated Crab)

serves **2** | prep **20 minutes, plus 24 hours to marinate** | cook **20 minutes**

When you think of eating crab, you don't normally think of eating it uncooked. This Korean recipe, called ganjang gejang, breaks that barrier. Normally, the recipe calls for blue crab, but around the West Coast of the US, blue crabs are not very common. Instead, we have Dungeness crabs, which are much bigger and meatier. Does this dish work with Dungeness crabs? Absolutely—by increasing the marination time, it comes out succulent and a perfect replica of the original dish. For teaching me how to make this dish, I have to give credit to Hazel, Dwight's wife—Dwight is one of my best friends and is also the artist behind the gyotaku (fish prints) throughout this book.

1 To dispatch the crabs, turn them on their backs. With a small paring knife, pry the "apron" of the crab down and stick the knife straight through the middle of the crab. The knife should go right under the apex of the apron. This is the most humane way to dispatch a crab. If you're uncomfortable with this method, you can place the crab in the freezer for 2 hours to put them to "sleep." In my opinion, this is the least humane method, as it takes a long time for the crab to be put to sleep.

2 Using a brush, scrub the crabs under cold water to clean off any gunk. It's up to you if you would like to keep the crab guts attached to the body and head. Next, quarter each of the crabs. Pull off the very tips of the crab legs to allow the marinade to penetrate all the way into the legs. Also pull off one side of the claw at the joint.

3 In a large saucepan, combine the sake and mirin. Bring to a simmer over medium-high heat, then use a lighter or a match to light a fire over the pan. Be careful, as the alcohol will go up in flames and start to burn off.

4 Separate the white and green parts of the green onions. Cut the white parts into 2-inch (5cm) pieces, and thinly slice the green parts, reserving the green parts for garnish.

5 Add the whites of the onions to the pan, along with the soy sauce, dashi, onion, garlic, ginger, jalapeños, and apple. Simmer for 20 minutes, then remove from the heat and allow the marinade to cool to room temperature.

6 Place the crab pieces in a large jar or food-safe container, and pour the cooled marinade over top. Marinate in the refrigerator for 24 hours.

7 To serve, use kitchen shears to cut into the crab legs and claws. Squeeze out the meat from the bodies. Enjoy the marinated crab over steamed rice, topped with the nori flakes, the reserved sliced green onion, and a drizzle of sesame oil.

2 live Dungeness crabs
1 cup (250ml) sake or soju
1 cup (250ml) mirin
1 bunch of green onions
5 cups (1.25L) soy sauce
5 cups (1.25L) dashi or water
½ yellow onion, quartered
6–8 garlic cloves, lightly crushed
1-in (2.5cm) piece ginger, sliced
1–2 jalapeños, sliced
1 apple or pear, quartered

To serve
Steamed white rice
Nori flakes
Sesame oil

Black Pepper Crab

serves **2–3** | prep **5 minutes** | cook **20 minutes**

This has become my go-to crab recipe. It's delicious and addictive and originally from Singapore. Shout out to all the viewers who insisted I try out this recipe years ago. Now I've developed my own recipe and have made it countless times. It's messy to eat but 100 percent a crowd pleaser. You can choose to incorporate the crab butter or omit. Some people are put off by the fact that it's crab guts, but others enjoy the richness it adds to the dish. Either way, this recipe is a banger.

1 To prepare the crabs, crack the claws and legs with the back of a knife. Some legs will be too soft to crack; for these, pull the very tips off the legs.

2 In a large wok or Dutch oven, heat the oil over medium-high heat. When hot, add the shallots and garlic and let sweat for 30 seconds. Add both the fine- and coarse-ground black pepper and butter. Stir for 30 seconds. Add the miso paste, oyster sauce, soy sauce, mirin, and 2 cups (500ml) water. Bring to a simmer.

3 Once the liquid reaches a simmer, add all the crab parts, including the head and guts, if using. Let the liquid return to a simmer, then cover and reduce the heat to low. Simmer, covered, for 12 minutes, removing the lid to stir occasionally.

4 Meanwhile, in a small bowl, combine the cornstarch and ½ cup (125ml) cold water, and mix well to make a slurry.

5 Using tongs, remove the crabs and set aside on a plate. Increase the heat to medium-high, and stir in the cornstarch slurry. Bring to a simmer, stirring frequently. Let the sauce simmer for 2 minutes or until it's thick enough to coat the back of a spoon.

6 When the sauce has thickened, pour over the crab. Garnish with cilantro, and enjoy with a side of rice or steamed buns. Dig in and get your hands dirty!

2 Dungeness crabs, uncooked, quartered (carapace/crab guts optional)

2 tbsp (30ml) cooking oil

1 shallot, thinly sliced

4 garlic cloves, minced

1 tbsp (8g) black pepper, fine ground

1 tbsp (8g) black pepper, coarse ground

4 tbsp (55g) butter

1 tbsp (15ml) white miso paste

2 tbsp (30ml) oyster sauce

1 tbsp (15ml) soy sauce

2 tbsp (30ml) mirin or 1 tbsp (12g) sugar

1 tbsp (8g) cornstarch

1 bunch of cilantro, chopped, to garnish

Cooked white rice or steamed buns, to serve

Scan for bonus content.

Crab Ramen

serves **4** | prep **30 minutes, plus at least 2 hours to rest dough and marinate eggs** | cook **30 minutes total**

This recipe incorporates all the goodness from the crab shells and guts to maximize the flavor of the ramen. First, you'll need to make fresh ramen noodles. They are just as easy to make as pasta and take about the same amount of time. The main difference is that the recipe for ramen noodles calls for sodium carbonate. This addition gives the noodles a bouncy texture. You can use a pasta maker to flatten the dough and cut into noodles, or you can roll it out with a rolling pin or wine bottle and slice into noodles by hand. It's ten times better than using dry ramen, so I encourage you to give it a shot.

The tare is the base layer of the broth, and a lot of other flavors can be infused into it. Adding the crab shells to the tare gives the final product a much stronger crab flavor. You can also add even more flavors by incorporating dried mushrooms, dried anchovies, kombu, and katsuobushi (bonito flakes).

Ramen eggs are simple as well, but I recommend preparing them 2 to 3 days in advance of making the full ramen recipe. The amount of time the eggs marinate will affect the creaminess and thickness of the yolks. Just a couple of hours of marination will not be enough time for the marinade to penetrate the yolks. After 24 hours, the marinade will fully saturate the egg whites. After 48 hours, it will reach the yolks, making them creamy and thick.

Boiling the noodles in the broth may seem like a good idea, but do not do this. There is too much starch in the fresh noodles, which will make the broth very gooey. Instead, boil the noodles in a separate pot of boiling water.

Noodles

1 Preheat the oven to 250°F (130°C). Sprinkle a thin layer of baking soda on a baking sheet. Place in the oven and bake for 1 hour. This will turn the baking soda (sodium bicarbonate) into sodium carbonate. Note that the pH level of sodium carbonate can cause skin irritation, so wearing food-safe gloves is recommended when handling.

2 In a small bowl, combine 2 teaspoons sodium carbonate with 1 cup (250ml) water. Stir until dissolved.

3 In a large bowl, combine the flour, salt, egg white, and sodium-carbonate water. Mix with a large spoon until a dough forms. It should look fairly dry, with some pieces of crumbs. If it doesn't, add a bit more flour.

4 With gloves on, roughly knead the dough to form a ball. It does not need to be perfectly smooth. Wrap with plastic wrap and let sit at room temperature for 30 minutes.

5 Dust a work surface with flour. Portion the dough into 4 pieces. Using a rolling pin, roll out a piece of dough to roughly 10 inches (25cm) in length. Fold into thirds, and roll it out again, this time perpendicular to the previous direction. Fold into thirds once more. Repeat with the remaining 3 pieces of dough. Cover with plastic wrap and let rest at room temperature for another 30 minutes.

6 Dust a work surface with flour again. Roll out the dough into several pieces, each 10 to 12 inches (25–30cm) in length. Transfer the dough to a pasta maker. Run the dough through the pasta maker multiple times, going from the thickest setting and working down to a thickness you like. Cut the noodles using the setting for spaghetti on the pasta maker.

7 Split the fresh noodles into 4 equal portions of about 5½ ounces (150g) each, and dust them with a sprinkle of cornstarch to keep from sticking. Wrap each portion in plastic wrap and keep refrigerated for up to 3 days or until ready to use. For longer storage, freeze for up to 3 months.

Crab Tare Sauce

1 Place a medium pot over medium heat. When hot, add the crab shells and toast for 5 minutes.

2 Add the sake and mirin. Bing to a simmer. Carefully light a match or lighter directly over the pot to burn off the alcohol. There will be a burst of flame, so do this cautiously with your face away from the pot. Keep it simmering low until the alcohol is completely burned off.

3 Add the soy sauce and crab butter. Simmer for 15 minutes.

4 Strain the sauce through a sieve and cheesecloth into a medium bowl or jar, and let cool. Use when cool, or store in the refrigerator for up to 5 days.

Ramen Egg

1 Fill a medium pot three-fourths full with water, and bring to a boil over high heat.

2 While the water is coming to a boil, prepare the eggs. Poke a small hole at the tip of the egg with a thumbtack. This allows air to release from the egg while boiling, creating perfectly round eggs that are easier to peel. Using a spoon, gently lower each egg, one at a time, into the boiling water. Reduce the heat to medium-low as it returns to a boil. Set a timer for 6 minutes 30 seconds.

3 When the timer expires, drain the boiling water, and add the eggs to a bowl filled with ice water. Once the eggs are cool to the touch, peel the shells.

4 Place the eggs in a large zipperlock bag and add the tare sauce, turning the eggs to coat. Place the eggs in the refrigerator to marinate for at least 2 hours or up to 2 days for best flavor.

Crab Shoyu Ramen

1 Fill a large pot three-fourths full with water, and bring to a boil over high heat.

2 Meanwhile, in a medium pot over medium-high heat, bring the dashi to a simmer.

3 While both pots are heating up, preheat two ramen bowls by filling them with hot water. Set aside.

4 When the water is boiling, add the fresh noodles and boil for 1 minute. Taste a noodle to check for doneness. Drain the noodles and set aside.

5 Discarding the hot water from the ramen bowls, and place 2 tablespoons (30ml) crab tare into each bowl, along with a pinch of the whites from the green onions and a spoonful of crab butter.

6 Into each ramen bowl, ladle piping-hot dashi, approximately 12 ounces (350ml) of broth. Place a portion of fresh ramen noodles into each bowl. Top with the crab meat and ramen eggs, and garnish with the green onions.

For the noodles

2 tsp (10g) baking soda

3⅓ cups (400g) all-purpose flour, plus extra for dusting

1 tsp (6g) salt

1 egg white

Cornstarch, for dusting

For the crab tare sauce

Shell from 1 medium or large crab

⅓ cup (75ml) sake

⅓ cup (75ml) mirin

½ cup (125ml) soy sauce

Crab butter (guts) from 1 crab

For the ramen egg

4 eggs

1½ cups (375ml) tare

For the crab shoyu ramen

6 cups (1.5L) dashi

4 portions of ramen noodles

1 cup (250ml) crab tare

1 bunch of green onions, chopped, white and green parts separated

1 or 2 crab carapace with crab butter

1½lb (675g) crab meat

4 ramen eggs, halved

Recipe image on following page.
→

Scan for bonus content.

Dungee Congee

serves **4–6** | prep **8 minutes** | cook **1 hour 10 minutes**

One of my favorite comforting camping meals is dungee congee. "Dungee" refers to Dungeness crab, but this recipe works with any crab meat. It does wonders on those cold nights outside. The recipe takes a bit of time, but it's so simple to make. I've made this dish many times, but the most memorable was when I was stuck in a cabin in Alaska with no electricity, cell service, or WiFi. Without all the distractions from our daily lives, it becomes obvious that one of the most important things in the moment is food. Just imagine it: a few friends, nobody else in sight, whales breaching in the distance, and this dungee congee. (If you don't believe me, there's a video on my YouTube channel of this exact moment.) The crab can be cooked prior to making this dish. If you would like to include the crab butter, boil the whole crab in salted water for 12 to 15 minutes. If you opt out of using the crab butter, simply clean the crab and steam for 10 to 12 minutes.

1. To a medium pot over high heat, add 8 cups (2L) water and bring to a boil. Add the rice, reduce the heat to low, and cover. Cook for 30 minutes, stirring occasionally.

2. Add the hondashi, salt, rice vinegar, ginger, shallot, garlic, pepper, crab carapace, and the whites of the chopped green onions. Cook for another 25 minutes.

3. Add the crab meat and unsalted butter, and salt to taste. Cook for 5 minutes.

4. Serve hot in a bowl and garnish with the greens of the chopped green onion, a drizzle of chili crisp, and red pepper.

1 cup (200g) medium- or short-grain rice, rinsed

2 tsp (10ml) hondashi or chicken bouillon

1 tsp (6g) salt

1 tsp (5ml) rice vinegar

2-in piece ginger, julienned

1 shallot, finely diced

4 garlic cloves, finely diced

1 tbsp (8g) fresh cracked black pepper

1 Dungeness crab carapace (the head with crab butter included)

1 bunch of green onions, chopped, whites and greens separated

½lb (225g) Dungeness crab meat, or any crab, cooked and shelled

1 tbsp (15g) unsalted butter

Salt, to taste

1 tbsp (15ml) chili crisp, to garnish

Sliced red chili pepper, to garnish

Scan for bonus content.

Crab Omurice

serves **4** | prep **20 minutes** | cook **20 minutes**

Omurice is a Japanese fried rice dish encased in an omelet. The Japanese style of making fried rice for this dish is with a tomato base, using ketchup and tomato paste. You'll find this dish all over Japan in different varieties, ranging from fancy French-style omelets to a simple egg blanket enclosing the rice. Traditionally, omurice is topped with ketchup, but I like to make a crab gravy to go with it instead. For that, you'll need to save the crab shells and simmer them in dashi or water, then add a cornstarch slurry to thicken the mixture to a gravy.

1   Peel the crab, removing any crab meat from the shell. Set the crab meat aside and reserve the shells.

2   In a medium saucepan over medium heat, toast the crab shells for 5 minutes. Then add the dashi and a pinch of salt. Simmer for at least 10 minutes. Strain the crab stock through a sieve to remove the shells, then return the stock to the saucepan.

3   In a small bowl, combine the cornstarch and ½ cup (125ml) cold water. Mix thoroughly to create a slurry. Stir the cornstarch slurry into the stock. Bring to a simmer over medium heat, stirring frequently. When the sauce has thickened, turn off the heat. Set aside.

4   In a wok, heat 1 tablespoon oil over high heat. When hot, add the onion and sauté for 30 seconds. Add the garlic, carrot, and tomato paste, and sauté for 30 seconds more. Toss in the day-old rice, breaking up any clumps as you mix it together. If the rice is dry, add another 1 tablespoon oil. Add the soy sauce, sesame oil, ketchup, sweet corn, and reserved crab meat. Cook for 3 to 5 minutes, mixing and stirring every minute.

5   While the fried rice cooks, heat the remaining 1 tablespoon oil in an large nonstick skillet over medium-high heat. Add the beaten eggs, spread them around the pan, and mix vigorously with a spatula for 20 seconds. Then stop and tilt the pan in each direction to spread across the pan again, making a crepe-like omelet. Cook for 2 to 4 minutes, depending on how runny or solid you like your eggs to be cooked.

6   To assemble the dish, fill a wide bowl with the fried rice and pack it down a bit. Flip the bowl upside down onto a larger plate, leaving the rice in a nice dome shape. Place the omelet on top and cover with the crab gravy. Garnish with chopped chives.

2lb (900g) whole crab, cooked
2 cups (500ml) dashi or water
Pinch of salt
1 tbsp (8g) cornstarch
2–3 tbsp (30–45ml) cooking oil
½ yellow onion, chopped
4 garlic cloves, chopped
1 carrot, chopped
1 tbsp (15ml) tomato paste
4 cups (225g) cooked day-old white rice
1 tbsp (15ml) soy sauce
½ tbsp (8ml) sesame oil
¼ cup (60ml) ketchup
½ cup (68g) sweet corn
4 eggs, lightly beaten
¼ cup (12g) chopped chives, to garnish

Scan for bonus content.

Spicy Raw Squid

serves **2–4** | prep **30 minutes** | cook **None**

Squid is one of my favorite seafoods, not only for its taste but also because squid is relatively sustainable. Most squid live for 6 to 10 months. They grow fast, reproduce, and then die, making them one of the most sustainable seafoods out there. In fact, the bigfin reef squid is the fastest growing marine invertebrate, and they can be caught in Japan, New Zealand, Australia, and other parts of the Indo-Pacific Ocean. In California and Washington, it is popular to catch market squid (small squid) in the ocean. Places like Monterey and Santa Cruz are squid hotbeds during the spring months. You can also catch them down in Southern California around the Channel Islands. Washington's squid season is in the summer to early fall, and squid there can be caught on many piers near Seattle at night. The best time is during the few days before and after the full moon.

1   Before you prepare and cook squid, be sure to clean it properly. It can be sliced into strips or rings.

2   **To slice into strips:** Cut down the middle of the tube to open and expose the inside of the squid. Remove the quill, and cut off the guts and discard. With smaller squid, the eyes can be squeezed out. With larger squid, make a slit in the eyes and then use your hands to remove them. In between all the legs, squid have a "beak" that can be removed with tweezers. Use a paper towel to remove the skin on the outside of the mantle. Slice the mantle into strips.

   To slice into rings: Find the V-shaped point on the front of the mantle, just above the eyes. Using tweezers, pinch the tip of the V and pull gently to remove the quill. If the quill breaks in the process, pinch through the mantle where you think it broke and pull it out through the mantle. Gently pull the leg portions away from the mantle to remove the guts. You may have to reach into the mantle with your fingers to clear out any remaining guts. Use the same process as above to remove the eyes, beak, and skin. Slice the mantle into rings.

3   Place the squid pieces in a small bowl and sprinkle lightly with salt. Mix together, and let sit for 15 minutes. Drain any excess liquid.

4   In a medium bowl, combine the green onions, ginger, gochujang, gochugaru, soju, honey, sesame oil, and soy sauce, and mix thoroughly. Add the sesame seeds and squid. Mix well once more, and serve.

1 whole squid, about 1lb (450g)

1 tsp (18g) salt

2 bunches of green onions, chopped

1-in (2.5cm) piece ginger, grated

3 tbsp (44ml) gochujang

1 tbsp (16g) gochugaru

1 tbsp (15ml) soju or sake

½ tbsp (8ml) honey

½ tbsp (8ml) sesame oil

½ tbsp (8ml) soy sauce

2 tsp (6g) toasted sesame seeds

Miso-Butter Scallop Salad

serves **2** | prep **10 minutes** | cook **5 minutes**

Did you know you can harvest scallops along the coast of California? These types of scallops are called rock scallops and are typically found around 10 feet (3m) or deeper. You can free dive for them from Southern California all the way up to Alaska. I harvested my first one on the jetty in Bodega Bay while diving for Dungeness crabs. They grow directly on rocks and blend in well with both the rocks and seaweed, but when they open their shell, they have bright orange "lips" that stick out from the environment like a sore thumb.

1 In a small bowl, combine the butter, miso, garlic, tarragon, and chives. Using a fork, mix thoroughly.

2 Place a large skillet over medium-high heat. Lightly salt each scallop. When the skillet is smoking hot, add the olive oil and place the scallops in a circle. Then, add a large spoonful of the compound butter. When the butter starts to bubble, tilt the pan, and with a spoon, baste the scallops. Cook for 2 to 3 minutes on one side only. Add 1 teaspoon lime juice to finish. Remove the scallops from the pan and set aside.

3 In a small bowl, combine the remaining miso butter from the pan and the remaining 1 teaspoon lime juice, as well as any liquid from the resting scallops to make the miso-butter sauce. Mix well.

4 In a serving bowl, combine the frisée lettuce, scallops, crunchy noodle toppings, and the miso-butter sauce. Garnish with lime zest.

4 tbsp (55g) butter, softened to room temperature

¼ cup (60ml) miso

4 garlic cloves, chopped

1 tbsp (1g) chopped tarragon

1 tbsp (3g) chopped chives

Pinch of salt

½lb (225g) jumbo sea scallops, about 6–8 scallops

1 tbsp (15ml) olive oil

2 tsp (10ml) lime juice

1 head frisée lettuce, leaves loosely separated

¼ cup (14g) crunchy noodle topping or croutons

Zest of 2 limes

Sea Urchins

Uni (sea urchin) is an expensive delicacy usually served in sushi restaurants, but if you harvest your own, enjoying uni is easy and doable for most people.

In California, all it takes is a negative tide to find sea urchins in tide pools. From the Sonoma Coast to Mendocino and Humboldt counties, purple urchins have become overly abundant due to a decline in the population of their top predator, a species of starfish called the sunflower sea star. Although purple urchins are native to the region, their exploding population growth has caused the number of kelp beds to decline, thus affecting the abalone and fish populations that depend on kelp for shelter and food.

So if sea urchins are abundant, why are they so expensive? The first reason is the labor it requires to collect sea urchins and process them. It's all done manually and takes time and effort. The second reason is because purple urchins are not considered to be commercial grade; they are simply too small to make a profit on. In California, there's another species called the red urchin, often referred to as Santa Barbara uni, which is gathered for commercial use. Red urchins are much bigger in size, and the yields are much higher. However, in my opinion, they are not as tasty as the purple urchins, which are sweet and delicious.

One way to tackle the overpopulation of purple urchins is by harvesting more of them, which is easy to do. They can be found in water as shallow as 2 feet (0.6m) or as deep as 30 feet (9m), mostly around rocky coastlines. Van Damme Beach in Mendocino is a perfect place for beginners to dive for urchins, and the locals will love you for targeting them! You can also search for purple urchins during low tide. Just about every beach in Mendocino will have sea urchins all over the tide pools.

Like California, New Zealand also has a sea urchin issue. The sea urchins there, aka kina, are creating an "urchin barren"—essentially a desert on the sea floor covered with urchins—leading to the same kelp issues that affect abalone and fish populations. This overabundance means urchins are just as easy to collect in New Zealand as they are in California.

Smoked Uni

yield **about 6 ounces (170g)** | prep **10 minutes** | cook **20 minutes**

Uni, aka sea urchin, has become very popular in the West but is still polarizing for many. This recipe, which was inspired by some friends in New Zealand, will blow your mind. If you already like uni, you'll love this dish—and if you're not sure about uni, you will be if you try this smoked uni.

1   Wearing gloves to protect your fingers from the spines, hold 2 large spoons back to back, and insert the tips of the spoons down and onto the teeth of the urchin. Push the spoons inward, then squeeze the spoon handles together to pry the urchin open, cracking it in half.

2   With your fingers, gently remove everything inside except the uni. You can also shake out the inside, as the uni will remain stuck. Use a spoon to scoop the uni out. Reserve the shells.

3   Place the uni in cold salt water. Clean the uni of any remaining impurities by hand. Then drain and place on a paper towel.

4   Return the cleaned uni to the now-empty shells.

5   Place the shells in a smoker, and smoke at a low temperature for at least 20 minutes. See page 89 for instructions on creating a makeshift smoker.

15–20 live sea urchins

Note
A fishing license is required to collect any seafood from the ocean in most of the US, except Hawaii. New Zealand does not require a license to fish or collect seafood from the ocean.

Scan for bonus content.

Okonomiyaki

serves **4–6** | prep **10 minutes** | cook **20 minutes**

Okonomiyaki is a savory Japanese pancake that's famous as street food in Osaka, which is where I was born and spent the first half of my childhood. I make this dish for a lot of my friends, and it's always a hit. *Okonomi* translates to "as you like," meaning there are infinite ways to customize it to your preference. I'm giving you my baseline recipe but don't be afraid to add your own flavors and ingredients. It's a great dish to clean out the fridge and use up any ingredients that need to go. The traditional okonomiyaki sauce, called okonomi, is easy to make at home. A store-bought version, made by Otafuku, can be found at most Asian markets.

1 To make the sauce, in a medium bowl, combine the Worcestershire sauce, ketchup, and oyster sauce. Mix well to combine, then set aside until ready to serve.

2 In a large bowl, combine the cabbage, green onions, flour, cornstarch, hondashi, eggs, salt, and 2 cups (500ml) cold water. Mix well so that the consistency is like pancake batter.

3 Heat a skillet over medium heat. When hot, ladle in the batter to create a pancake roughly 6 inches (15cm) in diameter. Place several pieces of raw squid on top. Cook for 8 minutes on one side, then flip it over and cook for another 6 to 8 minutes with the squid fully touching the hot skillet. To check if the okonomiyaki is cooked, push down on it occasionally; if you hear more of a sizzle, the pancake is still raw. When fully cooked, flip the okonomiyaki onto a plate. Repeat with the rest of the batter.

4 To serve, top each pancake with a drizzle of the okonomi sauce and Kewpie mayo and a sprinkling of katsuobushi.

For the homemade okonomi sauce

1 tbsp (15ml) Worcestershire sauce
½ cup (125ml) ketchup
½ cup (125ml) oyster sauce

For the okonomiyaki

1lb (450g) green cabbage, finely chopped
2 bunches of green onion, thinly sliced
1¼ cups (150g) all-purpose flour
2 tbsp (16g) cornstarch
½ tbsp (15ml) hondashi powder
4 eggs
2 tsp (12g) salt
2lb (900g) raw squid, cleaned
Kewpie mayo or regular mayo, to serve
Katsuobushi (bonito flakes), to serve

Note
Instead of using one whole green cabbage, you can also use ½ head of green cabbage and ½ head of purple cabbage for a bit more color. You can also speed up the cooking process by using a second skillet.

Scan for bonus content.

Scallop Pasta

serves **2** | prep **10 minutes** | cook **15 minutes**

The key to a well-cooked scallop is the sear. A nice browning is key to building flavor and caramelizing the sweetness of the scallop. Be sure to use a smoking-hot pan, and do not move the scallop once it's in the pan until it's ready to flip. In this recipe and in the photo, I use only three scallops per plate, but once sliced into pieces, they go a long way.

1. Place a medium pan or cast-iron skillet over medium-high heat. Using a paper towel, pat the scallops completely dry, then sprinkle salt on each scallop evenly, making sure to reserve some salt for the pasta water.

2. When the skillet is hot, add the oil. Place the first scallop on the skillet at the 12 o'clock position, pressing down firmly on the scallop for 5 to 10 seconds. Place the next scallop at the 2 o'clock position, and repeat until all scallops are on the skillet. Cook on the first side for 3 minutes or until you see a nice sear or browning on the bottom. Flip the scallops, starting with the scallop in the 12 o'clock position. Press down on the scallop firmly, using a spoon if it's too hot. Cook for another 3 minutes on the opposite side, then set aside on a plate.

3. Bring a large pot of water to a boil over high heat. Add the rest of the salt and the pasta, and cook according to package instructions, removing from the heat when the pasta is 1 minute away from reaching al dente. Drain, reserving ½ cup (125ml) pasta water, and set aside.

4. Place the skillet used for the scallops over medium heat. Add the onions, garlic, and 2 teaspoons cooking oil, if needed. Let the onions sweat for 1 minute, then deglaze by adding ¼ cup (60ml) pasta water and stirring for 1 minute more.

5. Add the heavy cream, Greek yogurt, and gochugaru, and stir to combine. Bring to a simmer. Stir the pasta into the sauce for 1 minute to finish cooking it. If the sauce seems too thick, add another ¼ cup (60ml) pasta water.

6. Using a sharp knife, slice each scallop into 4 pieces. Add any accumulated scallop juices to the pasta. Plate the pasta first and top with scallops and ikura, then garnish with microgreens.

6 scallops

1 tbsp (18g) salt, divided

1 tbsp (15ml) cooking oil, plus more as needed

10oz (280g) dry spaghetti

¼ yellow onion, finely diced

3 garlic cloves, chopped

¼ cup (60ml) heavy cream

2 tbsp (30g) plain Greek yogurt or sour cream

½ tbsp (8g) gochugaru

2 tbsp (30g) ikura (cured salmon roe)

¼ cup (20g) microgreens, to garnish

COASTAL PLANTS

Coastal Plants

I started learning about edible plants while attending San Francisco State University. I don't exactly remember why I became interested in foraging— maybe it was because I didn't have much money for groceries or perhaps it was just a genuine curiosity. I learned a lot from the first book about foraging I picked up: *The Bay Area Forager* by Kevin Feinstein and Mia Andler. At first, I became obsessed with learning if certain plants would give you nutrients and energy or if they would poison you. I soon realized there are so many weeds that are completely edible but that some can potentially kill you. It became a hobby to distinguish the edibility of plants while walking around the city, through parks, and in wilderness areas. Anytime I would be walking around with a friend, I felt the need to let them know if we were passing by edible or poisonous plants.

Harvesting edible weeds is like getting free groceries. You're most likely doing Mother Nature a favor by removing weeds, and at the same time, you're providing food for yourself. Not only are edible weeds abundant, but they actually taste good too. Even better, weeds grow without any direct input, and they are often more nutritious than any store-bought kale or other "superfoods." Just remember to stay away from harvesting edible plants from roadsides as they are often sprayed with herbicides and pesticides by the city to maintain the road. There are many invasive plants that taste good and that are easy to identify. I'll go through a few common invasive species in this chapter.

Baked Cod Medallions with Yuzu Hollandaise and Sea Asparagus

serves **4** | prep **10 minutes, plus 2 hours to marinate** | cook **20 minutes**

Sea asparagus goes by many names: marsh samphire, glasswort, pickleweed, and sea bean. I've seen them growing in many places, including the San Francisco Bay, Alaska, and New Zealand. They grow in subtropical to subarctic regions along coastal salt marshes. I've even found them cliffside along the open coast as I was climbing down to get to a fishing spot. They are very easy to identify, and luckily, there are no poisonous look-alikes.

Sea asparagus tastes as if it's been pickled in a salty brine. It has a nice snap and crunch and adds a burst of saltiness to any dish. Naturally, it pairs well with fish and citrus. I created this recipe with contrasting textures and complementary flavors.

1 To make the marinade, in a medium bowl, combine the miso, mirin, sesame oil, and lemon juice. Add the cod, turning to coat. Refrigerate for at least 2 hours.

2 Preheat the oven to 400°F (200°C). Line a baking sheet with parchment paper.

3 Remove the cod from the marinade, and place on the prepared baking sheet. Add the eggplant to the baking sheet, skin side down. Brush some of the miso marinade onto the eggplant, then sprinkle the sea asparagus over top. Bake for 15 minutes.

4 Meanwhile, prepare the yuzu hollandaise. Add the egg yolk to a medium glass or stainless steel mixing bowl. Place the bowl over a saucepan of simmering water, creating a double boiler. Whisk the egg yolk, and slowly add the melted butter while whisking until the mixture has emulsified. Add the yuzu juice and a pinch of salt. Mix until smooth.

5 Remove the eggplant, cod, and sea asparagus from the oven, and place the baking sheet on a cooling rack. Once cool, drizzle the hollandaise sauce over top, then garnish with lemon zest to serve.

1½lb (675g) cod filet, sliced into 2-in (5cm) sections
2 eggplants, quartered lengthwise and scored
2 cups (100g) sea asparagus
Zest of 1 lemon, to garnish

For the marinade
3 tbsp (45ml) miso
1 tbsp (15ml) mirin
1 tbsp (15ml) sesame oil
1 tsp (5ml) lemon juice

For the hollandaise
1 egg yolk
½ cup (110g) butter, melted
2 tsp (10ml) yuzu juice
Pinch of salt

Scallion Kimchi Pancakes with Invasive Three-Cornered Leek

makes **2 large pancakes** | prep **10 minutes** | cook **15 minutes**

These invasive three-cornered leeks can be found in much of the world. They grow as weeds in shady, wet areas and along ditches. As the name suggests, their stalks are triangular, making them easy to identify. They also have white flowers that droop downward. The smell is pleasantly oniony, milder and sweeter than a green onion. The entire plant can be eaten, from the bulbs to the flowers. You can pluck the entire plant or cut above the bulb. Peel off a couple of layers, as it's usually a bit dirty, then wash thoroughly under cold water before using.

This plant is extremely versatile in cooking so I decided to make Korean-style scallion pancakes replacing the scallions with three-cornered leeks. If the invasive plant is not available to you, you can use green onion in its place.

1 In a large bowl, combine all ingredients with 1 cup (250ml) water and mix well.

2 Heat a large nonstick or cast-iron skillet over medium heat. When hot, ladle a scoop of the mixture onto the pan to create a pancake roughly 1 inch (2.5cm) thick, pressing down as needed. Cook for 6 minutes on one side, then flip and cook for another 6 to 8 minutes. Repeat with the remaining batter.

3 Serve on a plate with an extra side of kimchi.

3 cups (300g) invasive three-cornered leek, cut into 2-in (5cm) segments
1 cup (170g) kimchi, chopped, plus extra to serve
1 cup (120g) all-purpose flour
1 tbsp (8g) cornstarch
1 tsp (7g) kosher salt
1 tbsp (7g) Korean chili flakes
1 tbsp (15ml) sesame oil
½ tbsp (5g) sesame seeds
2 eggs

Scan for bonus content.

Stinging Nettle Udon

serves **2** | prep **1 hour, plus 1 hour to rest dough** | cook **25 minutes**

Stinging nettles can be found in many places, like in gardens, along streams, in the woodlands, and elsewhere. They usually grow in shaded areas and in big patches. They inflict a sting upon touch, as the name suggests, so be careful when handling fresh stinging nettles. The stingers can be neutralized by cooking or crushing the leaves. A quick blanch is another great method.

One of the easiest noodles to make is Japanese udon. The thick noodles go well in soups and stir-fries. It's traditionally made with only three ingredients: flour, salt, and water. In this recipe, I add stinging nettles to create bright-green noodles. The nettle adds an herby, green-tea–like flavor to the noodles.

1 Bring a medium pot of water to a boil over high heat. Place 2 stalks of stinging nettles in the boiling water for 10 seconds, then remove from the heat and transfer to an ice bath. Strain out the blanched nettles after 1 minute. Set aside.

2 To the still-hot nettle water, add the kombu and katsuobushi and steep for 10 minutes in the residual heat. After 10 minutes, strain out the kombu and bonito flakes, and place the pot with the broth back over medium heat. Bring to a simmer, and add the fresh nettle leaves from the remaining 1 to 2 stalks of stinging nettles, reserving 8 to 10 leaves for frying. Remove the broth from the heat and set aside until ready to serve.

3 To a blender, add the blanched nettles, salt, and ½ cup (125ml) cold water. Blend for 10 to 15 seconds.

4 In a large bowl, combine the all-purpose flour and the blended nettle mixture. Using chopsticks or a fork, mix the flour into a dough. Once a dough has formed, transfer it to a worksurface, dust the worksurface with flour, and knead the dough for 5 minutes. Cover and let rest for 30 minutes.

5 After the dough has rested, place it in a large resealable plastic bag and knead by stepping on it over and over again (this is how it's traditionally made) for 5 to 10 minutes. Let rest in the bag for another 30 minutes. On a worksurface dusted with flour, roll out the dough to a ¼ inch (6mm) thick. Cut it into ¼ inch (6mm) wide noodles. Dust the noodles with the cornstarch to prevent them from sticking together, reserving 1 tablespoon (8g) cornstarch for the next step. Set the fresh noodles aside.

6 In a small saucepan, heat the oil over medium-high heat. While the oil heats up, combine the remaining 1 tablespoon (8g) cornstarch with ¼ cup (60ml) cold water, and mix well create a slurry. Dip the reserved nettle leaves one at a time into the slurry and then add them to the hot oil. Fry the nettle leaves for 30 to 45 seconds each, then transfer to a cooling rack. After the leaves are fried, use a fork to scoop bits of cornstarch slurry into the hot oil to create small, crunchy balls. Fry for 30 seconds or until golden brown. Repeat until you have about ¼ cup of crispy balls.

7 Place the broth prepared in step 2 over medium heat and bring to a simmer to prepare for serving.

8 Bring a medium pot of water to a boil over high heat. Add the fresh noodles and cook for 3 to 4 minutes, then drain.

9 To serve, divide the freshly cooked udon noodles between 2 bowls. Pour the hot broth over top, and garnish with the fried nettle leaves, crispy balls, green onion, and togarashi, if using.

3–4 stalks of stinging nettles, divided

¼ cup (7g) kombu (dried kelp)

2 cups (24g) katsuobushi (bonito flakes)

1 tsp (3g) salt

1 cup (120g) all-purpose flour, plus more for dusting

¼ cup (30g) cornstarch

½ cup (125ml) canola oil

¼ cup (25g) chopped green onion, to garnish

1 tsp (3g) shichimi togarashi (Japanese 7 spice; optional)

Seaweed and Kelp

Kelp is a valuable organism in the ocean, providing food and shelter for fish and shellfish. It also has the ability to absorb carbon dioxide from the ocean, helping to fight ocean acidification. In a place like Alaska where the summer days last over 20 hours, kelp can grow 12 inches per day. Kelp drop their spores yearly and grow to their full size of over 100 feet in a single year, making kelp a sustainable resource to provide food, energy, and renewable packaging. Kelp farms can grow without fertilizer, fresh water, or land and need minimal input to maintain. All these factors make kelp a valuable resource in our ecosystem.

Kelp has been used in Japanese cuisine for thousands of years for its umami properties and health benefits. In Japan, kelp is known as kombu. It is harvested and dried before use. Adding kombu along with bonito flakes is the method to make the Japanese soup stock called dashi, which can be added to soups and sauces for an amazing depth of umami. A small Alaskan company called Barnacle Foods has revolutionized the use of kelp in Western sauces, creating a market of kelp lovers across the US. They make hot sauces, salsas, barbecue sauce, and other seasonings. I teamed up with them to create Kelp Chili Crisp.

I first learned of Barnacle Foods on Instagram in 2019 from an ad for their kelp pickles. I loved the idea and reached out to them to ask if they minded if I made a video harvesting kelp and making my own version of the kelp pickles. The founders, Matt and Lia, were extremely excited and said it was not an issue. After that, we kept in touch, and my partner, Jocelyn, and I planned on visiting them one day in Alaska. In the summer of 2021, Jocelyn and I turned that dream into reality, driving from San Francisco, California, to Juneau, Alaska, in our converted Sprinter van. As soon as we made it to Alaska and met Matt and Lia in person, we hit it off. They took us to remote cabins to fish for big Pacific halibut and salmon, and we went harvesting for wild strawberries. We took full advantage of the long summer days and cooked amazing meals outdoors. Naturally, as we have common interests in food, travel, and the outdoors, we became good friends. Toward the end of that trip, they

asked me to collaborate on a kelp seasoning and asked me what I would want to create. That's where the idea for Kelp Chili Crisp was born.

We began our first trial of Kelp Chili Crisp on that trip to Juneau. We did it outdoors, heating the oil over a live fire. Then it started to rain. In a collective effort, we held skunk cabbage over the hot oil to avoid getting rain in it. You can probably imagine how well that worked—luckily, it wasn't heavy rain. Through some adversity, we completed our first trial of Kelp Chili Crisp and used it to cook our wild-caught salmon. It was delicious, but we all knew it could be even better. Over the next year, we worked on several variations, playing with different ingredients and recipes. We collaborated and shared the recipes we created that we thought were best.

In the summer of 2022, Jocelyn and I drove back up to Juneau, where we had a sample of the final five recipes to taste and compare. We finalized the recipe then and made our first batch of 100 jars. The Barnacle team scaled the production, and we finally launched our Kelp Chili Crisp to the country. Since the launch, we have received amazing feedback from people, and it is great to read how much people love it on the Barnacle Foods website. The best part is I always have a supply of chili crisp wherever I go.

Kelp Burger

makes **3–4 burgers** | prep **20 minutes** | cook **20 minutes**

I first posted this recipe in March 2021 on a YouTube video. The top comment on that video reads, "I wish Taku [would create] the Outdoor Chef Life cookbook." It was not something I had considered before, but the thought of creating my own cookbook was in the back of my mind from that day forward. The only thing holding me back was the amount of work that it would require. Fast forward a few years later, and Alex from DK (my publisher) reached out to me about writing a cookbook. This was my chance to make that comment come true. I sit here now, toward the tail end of finishing this cookbook, and I can say, although it took a lot of work, I'm happy to be able to finally share this with everybody who supported me throughout the years.

1 Bring a medium pot of water to a boil over high heat. Tenderize the kelp by boiling it for 3 to 4 minutes, then strain. Using a sharp knife, finely chop the kelp.

2 In a large bowl, combine the chopped kelp, mashed sweet potato, mushrooms, black beans, pepper, chipotle chili, salt, and panko, and then mix.

3 Grab a handful of the mixture and form a 1-inch-thick patty. Dust the outside with cornstarch. Set aside and repeat until all the mix is used up.

4 Heat a large cast-iron pan over medium-high heat. Add the oil. Once the pan has preheated for 3 minutes, add the kelp burgers. Cook 2 to 3 at a time so as to not crowd the pan. Cook on the first side for 4 to 5 minutes. Flip the burgers and lightly press the burgers into the pan using a spatula. Cook for an additional 4 to 5 minutes.

5 Once all the burgers are cooked, set them aside and turn off the heat. Warm the buns in the same pan using the residual heat.

6 To build the burger, start with the bottom half of a brioche bun. Layer on the kelp burger, ketchup, mustard, kelp pickles, onion, tomatoes, lettuce, and avocado. Top with the other half of the bun.

1lb (450g) fresh kelp or 4oz (110g) dried kelp

1 cup (200g) sweet potato, cooked and mashed (approximately 3–4 small sweet potatoes)

¼ cup (25g) mushrooms, chopped

1 cup (175g) black beans, chopped

1 tsp (7g) black pepper

1 tsp (7g) chipotle chili pepper powder

1 tsp (7g) salt

¼ cup (40g) panko breadcrumbs

½ cup (80g) cornstarch

2 tbsp (30ml) cooking oil

3–4 brioche buns

2 tbsp (30g) ketchup

2 tbsp (30g) mustard

½ cup (80g) kelp pickles

½ white onion, sliced

1–2 tomatoes, sliced

4–5 pieces lettuce, separated

2 avocados, sliced

Scan for bonus content.

Kelp Pickles

makes **about 4 cups (900g)** | prep **15 minutes** | cook **5 minutes**

Back in 2019, I came across an ad on Instagram from an Alaskan company called Barnacle Foods promoting their kelp pickles. I reached out to them to ask if I could recreate it and post it up on my YouTube channel. They were stoked about the idea. One day, while I was walking along the coast, I stumbled upon a washed-up piece of bull kelp. I knew it was fresh because it was shiny and clean, and it snapped when I bent it in half. This would be perfect to make kelp pickles.

1 Bring a large pot of water to a boil over high heat. Add the kelp and boil for 30 seconds. Strain, and then transfer the kelp to an ice bath. Once cooled, strain again and set aside.

2 In a medium pot, combine the vinegar, 2 cups (500ml) water, the salt, sugar, and peppercorns. Bring to a simmer over medium-high heat, and stir until the salt and sugar have dissolved. Once dissolved, remove from the heat.

3 To two 16-ounce (500ml) jars, evenly divide the kelp, garlic, and habaneros, alternating ingredients. Pour the hot vinegar mixture over the kelp, filling the jars to the top.

4 Seal the jars, and allow to cool on the counter.

2lb (900g) bull kelp stipe, thinly sliced

2 cups (500ml) distilled vinegar

1 tbsp (15g) kosher salt

½ tbsp (6g) cane sugar

10 whole peppercorns, lightly crushed

8 garlic cloves, sliced

2 habanero peppers, sliced

Note

Kelp pickles keep in the refrigerator for up to 4 to 6 months. They're delicious on avocado toast and sandwiches or chopped up in tartar sauce.

Scan for bonus content.

Seaweed Paste

makes **about 8 ounces** | prep **10 minutes** | cook **7 minutes**

In Japan, condiments for rice are everything. We have so many topping options for rice, but the only one that's really known in the United States is furikake. In my opinion, another one that should be more popular is nori paste, otherwise known as gohan desuyo. Kids in Japan go crazy for this stuff, and I, too, was one of those kids. It's really easy to make from scratch, and a huge benefit of this dish is that seaweed is a superfood.

For this recipe, you can use either freshly harvested nori seaweed from the coast or store-bought dried nori sheets like the ones used to make sushi. If using fresh seaweed, it's important to thoroughly clean it as freshly harvested seaweed will likely have small ocean critters. Give the seaweed a rinse under cold water at least two or three times. Don't worry too much if you don't get them all; the first step will take care of any you missed.

1 Bring a large pot of water to a boil over high heat. Add the seaweed and boil for 2 minutes to tenderize the seaweed and kill any sea critters. Strain the seaweed.

2 To a medium saucepan, add the seaweed, soy sauce, mirin, dashi, salt, and sugar. Bring to a simmer over medium heat and let simmer for 5 to 6 minutes, stirring every minute or so to make sure it doesn't burn. Remove from the heat and let cool.

3 Transfer the seaweed mixture to a blender, and blend until a paste is formed.

1lb (450g) fresh seaweed, or 10–15 sheets of dried nori, crumbled
1 tbsp (15ml) soy sauce
1 tbsp (15ml) mirin
1 cup (250ml) dashi
1 tsp (6g) salt
2 tsp (4g) sugar

Options For Serving

- **Seaweed paste on rice:** The most common way to enjoy seaweed paste is over freshly cooked rice. To do so, take about a spoonful of paste and spread it over the top of a bowl of rice.

- **Avocado toast with seaweed paste:** On the bread of your choice, evenly spread a generous helping of paste across the top. Lay sliced avocado over it, and top with a squeeze of Kewpie mayo. Bake at 350°F (180°C) for 6 minutes.

- **Cucumber salad with seaweed paste:** In a bowl, combine thinly sliced cucumber, seaweed paste, 1 tsp sesame oil, and a sprinkle of toasted sesame seeds. Mix together and serve.

Note
Store seaweed paste in a jar in the refrigerator for up to 2 weeks.

Kombujime (Kelp-Cured Fish)

serves **4–6** | prep **10 minutes, plus 2 hours to marinate** | cook **None**

Kombujime is a traditional Japanese technique that infuses the umami of the kelp into fish, which is then served as sashimi. This technique is typically used for white fish, like flounder and snapper. Many types of white fish are safe to eat raw, straight out of the ocean. In most cases, small and medium fish are going to have fewer parasites, but it also depends on species and diet. A fish like opaleye will normally be free of parasites because its diet consists mostly of seaweed.

1 Take a piece of cloth and dampen it with sake. Use the sake-dampened cloth to wipe the dried kelp clean.

2 Coat the filet evenly with the kosher salt, as though you are seasoning it to cook. Wrap the filet with kelp, making sure it has contact on all sides. Wrap the entire fish with a paper towel and then with plastic wrap. Refrigerate for 2 hours to marinate.

3 Unwrap the filet, and pat dry with a fresh paper towel. Slice into sashimi pieces, and serve with wasabi and soy sauce.

¼ cup (60ml) sake
½lb (225g) dried kelp
2lb (900g) flounder, halibut, or snapper filet
¼ cup (56g) kosher salt
Wasabi, to serve
Soy sauce, to serve

Seaweed Crisps

serves **2** | prep **20 minutes** | cook **25 minutes**

Have you ever had those delicious seaweed snacks? Most people probably have. They're salty, crispy, and tasty, and they're very easy to make with fresh seaweed. There are three main types of seaweed I would use for this: nori, sea lettuce, or wakame. All can be found during low tide on the Pacific Coast. Sea lettuce and nori are higher in the intertidal zone, meaning you can find them during most low tides. Wakame is found in deeper water. When harvesting seaweed, use a sharp pocketknife or scissors to cut close to the base of the seaweed instead of pulling it out entirely. This will help conserve the seaweed and allow it to grow back. If harvesting your own seaweed is not an option, you can use store-bought dried wakame sold in Asian markets (see page 44).

1 Bring a large pot of water to a boil over high heat. Add the fresh seaweed and blanch for 30 seconds to neutralize any sea critters. Strain the seaweed, and then spread out on a wire rack to dry for 30 minutes.

2 Preheat the oven to 160°F (71°C) or the grill to a low heat.

3 In a medium bowl, add the blanched and dried seaweed, sesame oil, sesame seeds, and salt. Mix well to incorporate.

4 Directly to the wire rack in the oven, lay the seaweed out in a single layer, and place a baking tray on the rack underneath it to catch any drippings. Sprinkle sea salt and sesame seeds over the seaweed, and bake for 25 minutes or until dry and crunchy.

1lb (450g) fresh seaweed (nori, sea lettuce, or wakame), or dried wakame, rehydrated (see note)

2 tbsp (30ml) sesame oil

1 tbsp (10g) sesame seeds, plus extra for sprinkling

1 tsp (6g) sea salt, plus extra for sprinkling

Note
Wakame can be bought in Asian markets as a dried ingredient. Simply rehydrate in hot water and use the same as you would fresh seaweed.

Seaweed Salad

serves **3–4** | prep **20 minutes** | cook **None**

People often ask me what types of seaweed are edible, and technically, they all are. There is no known seaweed that is poisonous, but some are tough, chewy, or just unpleasant to consume. They can be eaten straight off the rocks in the ocean, just like veggies in a garden, but cooking them, in my opinion, gives them a better texture. Seaweed doesn't need to be cooked long—just a minute or two in boiling water will make them more tender. Even though seaweed grows in salt water, it doesn't taste overly salty. Most have a nice briny flavor, but some are bland and pair great with salad dressings.

1 If using kombu (dried kelp), rehydrate by soaking in hot water for 5 minutes. (Do not boil.) If using fresh seaweed, blanch in boiling water for 2 minutes, then transfer to an ice bath to cool.

2 Drain the seaweed, and place it in a medium bowl.

3 In a separate medium bowl, combine the soy sauce, mirin, rice vinegar, dashi, sesame seeds, and lemon juice. Mix well.

4 Pour the marinade over the seaweed. Let sit for at least 10 minutes, and then serve.

2oz (55g) kombu or
   1lb (450g) fresh seaweed
1 tbsp (15ml) soy sauce
1 tbsp (15ml) mirin
2 tsp (10ml) rice vinegar
2 tbsp (30ml) dashi
½ tbsp (5g) toasted sesame
   seeds, crushed
1 tsp (5ml) lemon juice

WILD MUSHROOMS

Wild Mushrooms

The number one rule with wild mushrooms is do not eat them unless you are 100 percent confident of the identification. With that said, there are plenty of easy-to-identify wild mushrooms, like chanterelles, king boletes, morels, and several more. These are also considered to be top-choice mushrooms. There isn't one magical identifier to tell if a wild mushroom is edible or poisonous, but multiple factors can help you correctly identify mushrooms that are safe to eat.

Cap: The caps are the tops of the mushrooms and can be round, vase-shaped, cone-shaped, rough, smooth, or even slimy. Caps are the first thing you see, and they usually don't tell a mushroom's whole story, but they give a small clue into its identification.

Gills: Many mushrooms have paperlike gills under their caps, but some do not have gills at all. Chanterelles have veins, which are similar to gills but are more like ridges that split and taper down to the stem. Boletes have sponge-like pores instead of gills. Knowing these differences is key to successfully identifying each mushroom. However, solely knowing the type of gills will not help determine if the mushroom is edible. You must identify further.

Stem: Mushroom stems can be thick or thin, hollow or solid. It is important to see if the gills attach to the stem or stop short of the stem. The stem can also have what's known as a veil or a partial veil, which is a ring toward the top of the stem. All these characteristics help narrow down the identity of a mushroom.

Texture: Many choice mushrooms are often dense and firm. This alone will not constitute an edible mushroom, but it helps give a good clue.

These four identifiers are the most telling signs for correctly identifying mushrooms. There are several other identifiers too, like smell, color change or bruising, spore print, and growth medium. I suggest consulting a mushroom-identification book such as *Mushrooms of the Redwood Coast* by Noah Siegel and Christian Schwarz or *All That the Rain Promises and More* by David Arora to learn the identification process and how to get a visual of each characteristic. Then, it's as simple as getting out into the woods and looking for mushrooms to try identifying. You'll likely find many that are not mentioned in a guidebook, and that's okay. If you can't find the mushroom in the book, it is likely not edible. Keep moving, and look for more to identify. There are also look-alikes for some species, which can cause confusion. For example, jack-o'-lantern mushrooms and false chanterelles look very similar to golden chanterelles, but you can examine key identifiers like the gills to differentiate the poisonous from the prized.

Wild mushrooms can be found in much of the world, but I have the most experience foraging along the West Coast of the United States, from the Bay Area of California to southeastern Alaska. Mushroom season in Alaska starts much earlier than in California as Alaska experiences more rain and colder temperatures earlier in the seasons. There, you can expect to find chanterelles and king boletes as early as August and September. In Washington and Oregon, the best months for mushroom foraging are September and October. In California, aim to hunt for mushrooms closer to November and December.

I do most of my mushroom foraging within a few miles of the coast. Coastal areas provide cooler temperatures and moist environments, both of which play a crucial role for mushroom growth. One of the keys to success is to know what kinds of trees mushrooms prefer since trees are much easier to spot and identify than mushrooms. Knowing this for the specific mushroom you're after can help you greatly. The most important thing of all is timing. You can be in the best mushroom spot, but you'd never know it if you were there at the wrong time. Rain is important as well; wait at least a few days after a rainfall for the mushrooms to pop up.

Finding success with mushroom foraging is all about piecing together these clues. If you can do that, you'll be successful anywhere you go.

Scan for bonus content.

Mushroom Hauls

The feeling of accomplishment when you finally find a good haul of wild mushrooms after extensive research is a mix of excitement and satisfaction. It's a true testament to the knowledge you've gained watching tutorials, reading books, and learning about mushroom identification. If you get out there on a consistent basis, you're bound to have days where you find way too many to eat within a week. So what do you do when you have too many to eat? You can always share your haul with family and friends, or you can preserve the mushrooms to extend their shelf life. Here are some preservation methods I like to use.

Dehydrating Mushrooms

The most common method to preserve mushrooms is by dehydrating them with a dehydrator. The process removes all the moisture in the mushroom and dries them out. This is great not only for preserving but also for enhancing the mushroom flavor. Slice the mushrooms roughly ¼ inch (6mm) and dehydrate at 110°F (45°C) for 8 to 16 hours, depending on the mushroom. When fully dried, the mushroom should feel hard and dry. This works well for mushrooms like boletes, morels, shiitake, and trumpets, which develop a strong umami flavor and incredible smell.

Freezing Mushrooms

The second method is freezing the mushrooms. It's possible to freeze them as is, but it is better to freeze them after they're cooked. Slice your mushrooms ¼ inch (6mm) thick. You'll want 8 tablespoons (120g) butter for every 1 pound (450g) fresh mushrooms. Add the sliced mushrooms to a medium pan over medium heat, and allow them to release their moisture. Simmer until all the water has evaporated, about 5 to 10 minutes. Add the butter and cook for 3 to 4 minutes more. Remove from the heat and transfer to a plate to cool. Once cooled, portion the mushrooms into freezer bags, and store in the freezer. Use within a year.

Pickling Mushrooms

The third method is to pickle the mushrooms. Yes, pickled mushrooms are delicious! This process works great with chanterelles and allows the mushrooms to keep their amazing texture. You can use the finished product on top of cheese and crackers, in sandwiches, and with any other food that needs a kick of acidity.

To make pickled mushrooms, you'll want to start with 1 pound (450g) fresh mushrooms. Break the mushroom caps in half and pull apart the mushrooms into 4 to 6 strips each. In a medium pan over medium heat, dry sauté the mushroom strips for 4 to 8 minutes to release and evaporate the moisture. Set the mushrooms aside. In a small saucepan over medium heat, combine 1 cup (250ml) distilled vinegar, 2 cups (500ml) water, ½ tablespoon (9g) salt, and ½ tablespoon (6g) cane sugar. Bring to a low simmer, stirring until all the salt and sugar have dissolved. Then remove from the heat. In a clean glass jar with a lid, combine the sauteed mushrooms; ¼ onion, sliced; 6 garlic cloves, lightly crushed; and if desired, 1 habanero pepper, sliced. Pour the hot vinegar mixture into the jar, filling it to the top. Secure the lid, and allow it to cool on the counter for a few hours. Keep refrigerated for 2 to 4 months.

Matsutake Mushrooms

The pine mushroom, more commonly known as matsutake, is my G.O.A.T. mushroom. I would describe the flavor as more adult, mature, and foresty. It has a pleasantly fresh texture, but the greatest attribute of the matsutake is its fragrance. Matsutake is often described as smelling like spicy gym socks or Red Hots candy. I admit it does have a musky scent, but I wouldn't call it gym socks. Whatever it smells closest to, its aromatic nature gives it one of the most unique characteristics in the fungi kingdom.

The matsutake is a highly prized mushroom in Japan and is extremely expensive—not to mention, it's available only in the fall. The ones I have eaten have all been from the West Coast, specifically in California from Marin County to Mendocino County, where I've had the most luck finding them from late November to January. Look for tan oak forests with huckleberry. I've often found these treasures of the woods hidden under the huckleberry plants, just starting to emerge from the dirt. They can be incredibly difficult to spot.

The best advice I have to offer you is to look for "suspicious bulges" (as my partner, Jocelyn, calls them) in the dirt.

On one of our early days of mushroom foraging, we went out on a short recon mission to look for new spots, and Jocelyn ended up finding three matsutake right next to the trail. That's her kind of luck! These mushrooms are good hiders, so pay close attention, and you might just find the best mushroom the forest has to offer. In this section, you'll find a couple of my favorite matsutake recipes.

Scan for bonus content.

Matsutake Rice

serves **4–6** | prep **5 minutes** | cook **30 minutes**

The best way to prepare matsutake is with simple and mild flavors to contrast the strong, distinct mushroom taste. Super simple recipes are best, such as quartering and spraying with sake, then grilling. My favorite, though, has to be this rice dish. The mushroom is cooked together with the rice, infusing it with matsutake aroma. Even with a single matsutake, the fragrance alone will take over the rice. Matsutake mushrooms can be found in Japanese markets from the fall to early winter.

1 In a medium bowl, wash the rice under cold water 3 to 5 times. Strain all the rice into a sieve. Set aside.

2 In a separate medium bowl, combine the dashi, soy sauce, and mirin.

3 To a medium pot, add the rice and the dashi mixture. Layer the sliced matsutake over the surface and cover with a lid. Place over medium-high heat for 10 minutes or until it starts to boil. Once boiling, reduce the heat to low and cook for 10 to 12 minutes more.

4 After a total cook time of 20 minutes, increase the heat to medium-high for 15 to 20 seconds to slightly char the bottom. Turn off the heat and let rest for 10 minutes to finish the cooking process with the residual heat. Be sure to keep the lid on the pot for the entire cooking process.

5 Once the rice is cooked, add the chopped cilantro stems and lime zest. Fluff the rice and mix. Serve with cilantro leaves and a lime wedge as garnish.

2 cups (400g) short-grain white rice

2½ cups (625ml) dashi

1 tbsp (15ml) soy sauce

1 tbsp (15ml) mirin

2–3 medium matsutakes, wiped clean and thinly sliced into 6–8 pieces per mushroom

1 bunch of cilantro, chopped, stems and leaves separated

Zest of 1 lime

Lime wedges, to garnish

Note

I'm using cilantro stems in place of mitsuba, which is what I would normally use. Mitsuba is a difficult herb to get your hands on if you aren't near a major city with a good Japanese market. Cilantro stems are a good substitute.

Clear Matsutake Soup with Clams

serves **4–6** | prep **5 minutes** | cook **10 minutes**

Here is a simple recipe to complement the matsutake rice. A clear soup makes for a perfect, decadent broth. The clams add a lovely seafood flavor that pairs well with the soup. Both matsutake and clams can be harvested along the coast in late fall. Target the matsutake in the morning while the tide is high. Then head out to the coast for the afternoon low tide to harvest the clams.

1   In a medium pot, combine 8 cups (2L) water and the mushrooms. Bring to a simmer over medium-high heat. Simmer for 5 minutes, and then add the clams. Simmer for 5 minutes more or until all the clams have opened.

2   Add the lime juice and a pinch of salt. Taste and adjust seasoning as needed.

3   Serve garnished with cilantro.

2 medium matsutake, cleaned and very thinly sliced
1lb (450g) steamer clams in the shell
½ tsp (2.5ml) lime juice
Salt, to taste
Chopped cilantro, to garnish

Morel Mushrooms

Hunting for morel mushrooms has become a tradition for me and Jocelyn every spring. During the months when the mountains start to emerge from the winter season and the snow starts to melt, morels start to pop up. We've gathered them in Oregon and California, but they are widespread around the world. The most productive places are areas where there have been wildfires. Any kind of disturbance allows morels to grow, but burned areas are the most obvious places to spot them due to the burn marks on the trees. Another key criterion is finding south-facing hillsides. These sides of the mountain are most exposed to sunshine, which melts snow quicker and allows the mushrooms to grow. Finding the right elevation is another important aspect. If you're walking in snow, the elevation is likely too high for morel growth. If you see no snow at all, your elevation may be too low. Somewhere in between those altitudes seems to be the sweet spot.

In recent years, there have been instances of people eating morels with fatal consequences. A sushi restaurant in the Midwest served raw morels, which proved to be fatal for two customers and left 49 others feeling ill. To prevent this from happening to you, always cook morels thoroughly. I've provided a basic recipe next, which includes instructions on how to properly clean and cook these delicious mushrooms.

Scan for bonus content.

Sautéed Morels

serves **2–3** | prep **10 minutes** | cook **12 minutes**

There have been recent reports of people falling ill from eating uncooked morel mushrooms. In order to avoid any symptoms, morels need to be cooked well. My go-to method is to sauté them. Once properly cooked, morels can be added to different dishes like noodles, avocado toast, or mushroom congee (pictured).

1 With a sharp knife, slice the morels in half lengthwise to expose the cavity, which is sometimes filled with dirt. Rinse thoroughly under cold water, making sure to clean out all the nooks in the mushroom cap. Transfer to a paper towel and let dry.

2 Place the morels in a large nonstick skillet over medium heat (no oil). As they heat up, the morels will release most of their moisture. Once most of the moisture has evaporated, add the cooking oil, salt, garlic, and shallot. Cook for 4 to 5 minutes or until a slight crust develops on the mushrooms. Add the butter and thyme, and cook for another 2 to 3 minutes. Add to any dish!

1lb (450g) morels
1 tbsp (15ml) cooking oil
1 tsp (3g) salt
4 garlic cloves, chopped
1 medium shallot, chopped
4 tbsp (55g) unsalted butter
1 tsp (3g) minced fresh thyme

Morel Garlic Noodles

serves **2** | prep **10 minutes** | cook **15 minutes**

It's morel season as I write these recipes. Morels pop up every spring, and I have the best tips on how to find them. In my experience, they're always in burned forests with medium-to-light shade with recent snow mostly melted. In the early season, it's best to look around south-facing slopes, as they warm from the sun and melt the snow. You can look at past finds from people who have documented them on inaturalist.com to get a good clue of where they grow.

For this recipe, any mushrooms can be used. I've included the methods for dried mushrooms in step 1. If using fresh mushrooms, skip to step 2.

1 If using dried mushrooms, rehydrate by soaking the mushrooms in 2 cups (500ml) hot water for 5 to 10 minutes. Drain, reserving ¼ cup (60ml) of the mushroom water. Pat the mushrooms dry. (The rest of the mushroom water can be reserved for use in soups, if desired, or discarded.)

2 Bring a medium pot of water to a boil over high heat. Add the ramen noodles, and reduce the heat to medium. Cook for 1 to 2 minutes for fresh ramen, or according to package instructions for dried ramen. Drain and set aside.

3 In a large skillet or wok, heat the olive oil over medium heat. Add the mushrooms and cook for 3 to 4 minutes. Add the garlic and butter, and cook for 1 minute more. Stir in the soy sauce, oyster sauce, and fish sauce.

4 Add the reserved ¼ cup (60ml) of mushroom water. Transfer the cooked ramen noodles to the pan and mix them into the sauce. Add the chili flakes and green onions to finish.

1lb (450g) fresh morels or
  2–3 handfuls of dried morels
14oz (400g) fresh ramen
  noodles (page 162) or
  2 packages dried ramen
1 tbsp (15ml) olive oil
1 garlic head, chopped
4 tbsp (60g) butter
½ tbsp (8ml) soy sauce
1 tbsp (15ml) oyster sauce
½ tsp (2.5ml) fish sauce
1 tsp (3g) chili flakes
½ bunch of green onions,
  chopped

Chawanmushi
(Japanese Steamed Egg)

serves **2** | prep **10 minutes** | cook **30 minutes**

Chawanmushi is a small Japanese side dish. Its texture is silky smooth and light with a savory umami flavor. It's usually served in a smaller bowl than miso soup, but I think that's too small, so I make mine way bigger and use a wide ceramic bowl.

Chawanmushi pairs well with a variety of shellfish and mushrooms. Chanterelles or oyster mushrooms are perfect additions to this dish, which is what I suggest using for this recipe. I like to grill half of the mushrooms to use as toppings and cook the other half with the chawanmushi. The chawanmushi is best cooked in a tiered steamer, like the ones used for dumplings. Alternatively, you can achieve similar results using an oven. For this method, simply place the bowls on a baking sheet, cover with aluminum foil, and bake at 350°F (180°C) for 25 to 35 minutes or until the eggs are cooked.

1 Preheat the grill to 400°F (200°C).

2 In a medium bowl, whisk the eggs. Add the dashi, usukuchi, and mirin, and lightly whisk to combine. Cover and set aside.

3 With your hands, tear any large mushrooms in half. Keep the small and medium mushrooms whole.

4 Grill half of the mushrooms over medium-high heat for 2 to 3 minutes. Once the mushrooms start to sweat, brush them with soy sauce and chili oil. Continue to cook for 10 to 12 minutes, brushing the mushrooms 2 to 3 times more with soy sauce and chili oil. Transfer the grilled mushrooms to a plate, and set aside.

5 In a wide-bottomed ceramic bowl that can fit into a steamer, place the 4 peeled shrimp, 8 pieces of edamame, and 2 to 4 pieces of the reserved uncooked mushrooms. Pour the egg-dashi mixture over top, filling the bowl. Repeat with another bowl.

6 Bring a pot of water to a boil over high heat. Place the steamer onto the pot and set the ceramic bowls within. Cover and reduce the heat to low. Steam for 20 minutes. At the same time, steam the remaining 4 unpeeled shrimp for 10 minutes on the side. Let the bowls cool for 1 to 2 minutes, then top with the grilled mushrooms, the steamed shrimp, and chili oil. Serve hot.

4 eggs

2½ cups (625ml) dashi

1 tbsp (15ml) usukuchi (light soy sauce)

1 tbsp (15ml) mirin

½lb (225g) oyster mushrooms, divided

2 tbsp (25ml) soy sauce

1 tbsp (15ml) chili oil, plus more to serve

8 jumbo shrimp, 4 peeled and 4 unpeeled

¼ cup (40g) cooked, shelled edamame

Note
This dish can be prepared well in advance to just before the steaming stage. It's a great dish to serve as the last course of a meal.

Scan for bonus content.

Agedashi Mushroom Soba

serves **2** | prep **20 minutes** | cook **10 minutes**

This is another classic Japanese-style recipe. *Age* means "to fry" in Japanese, and *dashi,* as you may recall from earlier in this cookbook, is the broth. So *agedashi* translates to "frying in broth." A popular example is agedashi tofu, where the tofu is fried and placed inside the broth. It's lightly flavored but delicious and savory. For this recipe, we are replacing the tofu with mushrooms. You can use a variety of mushrooms, like oysters, king trumpets, chanterelles, hedgehogs, or chicken of the woods. Some wild mushrooms are waterlogged, meaning the mushrooms hold a lot of water. In this case, the mushrooms should be dry sautéed to remove the moisture before frying. To do so, heat a dry pan over medium heat and toss in the mushrooms without any oil. When the water has evaporated and the mushrooms have released their liquid, they are ready to fry.

1   In a large saucepan, preheat the oil over medium heat.

2   In a small bowl, combine half of the mochiko and ½ cup (125ml) water to make a thin batter. Toss the mushrooms into the batter. If using dry sautéed mushrooms, skip the water and coat with just cornstarch.

3   Gently place the battered mushrooms into the hot oil. Fry for 6 to 8 minutes or until golden brown. Remove the mushrooms and salt immediately. Let cool on a wire rack and set aside.

4   Bring a medium pot of water to boil over high heat. Once the water is boiling, add the soba noodles. Cook for 5 minutes or according to package instructions. Once cooked, dunk the noodles in an ice bath to stop the cooking process.

5   To serve, divide the soba noodles evenly between 2 bowls, add some mushrooms to each bowl, and pour 1 cup (250ml) cold dashi over top. Garnish with grated daikon and chopped green onions to finish. Serve hot or cold.

2 cups (500ml) canola or other frying oil

¼ cup (32g) mochiko flour or cornstarch

½lb (225g) mushrooms, in roughly 3-in (2.5cm) clumps

Generous pinch of salt

Two (200g) portions dry soba noodles

2 cups (500ml) cold dashi

½ cup (180g) grated daikon, to garnish

1 bunch of green onions, chopped, to garnish

Raw Porcini Mushrooms

serves **1–2** | prep **10 minutes, plus 30 minutes to rest** | cook **None**

Wild porcini mushrooms, aka king bolete mushrooms, are plump and dense with a cap that has the color of a freshly baked bun. Although they are considered prized mushrooms, they can be plentiful and easy to find. The best time to forage for porcini is in the fall after some rain. I've had the most success finding porcini where there is medium shade around pine trees. They seem to love the duff that the pine needles create. Small, fresh porcini usually hide really well under the duff.

To make this recipe, you'll need the younger, fresh porcini. You can usually tell how fresh the mushroom is by squeezing its stem. Young porcini are very firm and dense. Older specimens tend to be softer and, if you cut them open, they usually have evidence of bugs in them, which is perfectly fine once cooked or dehydrated, but not ideal to eat raw. Porcini make one of the best dehydrated mushrooms to create a soup stock. Give raw porcini a try if you ever come across a young one.

1 Arrange the sliced porcini in a single layer on a serving dish, and drizzle heavily with the olive oil. Let soak for at least 30 minutes.

2 Sprinkle the rest of the ingredients over top and enjoy fresh.

1–2 porcini mushrooms, very thinly sliced
¼ cup (60ml) olive oil
4–6 cherry tomatoes, halved
1 tbsp (6g) crushed cashews
1 tsp (1g) chopped chives
1 tsp (6g) flaky sea salt
Zest of 1 lemon

Note
Not all mushrooms are fit for raw consumption. This recipe must be made specifically with younger porcini mushrooms.

Scan for bonus content.

Mushroom Kimchi Risotto

serves **2** | prep **15 minutes** | cook **25 minutes**

Store-bought or cultivated mushrooms hold a lot less moisture than wild mushrooms because wild mushrooms sit out in the rain and absorb much of that water over the course of their lifespans. When cleaning mushrooms, some chefs will mention not to run them under water. I used to follow this rule of thumb, but in all honesty, it doesn't seem to make a difference with wild mushrooms. The thought of water ruining the texture, aroma, or flavor makes no logical sense to me when they get rained on in the wild. Cooking with wild mushrooms will typically require a dry sauté to draw out the moisture. With store-bought or cultivated mushrooms, there's no need to dry sauté.

1   In a large, dry skillet over medium heat, sauté half of the mushrooms for 2 to 5 minutes or until the moisture in the mushrooms has been drawn out and evaporated. Add 2 tablespoons (42g) butter. Season with the salt and pepper, and cook for 3 to 4 minutes more. Set aside.

2   In a medium pot, bring the chicken stock to a simmer over high heat. Once simmering, reduce the heat to low.

3   In a pot or large saucepan, heat the olive oil over medium-high heat. When the oil is hot, add the onion and the remaining mushrooms, and sauté for 1 to 2 minutes.

4   Add the arborio rice and stir for 30 seconds. Add the white wine and stir for 1 minute more.

5   Mix in the gochujang and 2 ladles of the hot chicken stock. Bring to a simmer, stirring the rice constantly, and then reduce the heat to medium. As the rice starts to absorb the liquid, continue to add the hot stock, 1 ladle at a time. Keep stirring constantly for 15 minutes, adding stock as the rice absorbs the liquid. Then stir in the kimchi, ½ cup (60g) Parmesan, and the remaining 3 tablespoons butter. Cook for another 3 to 5 minutes or until the rice is al dente.

6   Plate the risotto and top with sautéed mushrooms. Garnish with the remaining Parmesan and chives as desired.

1lb (450g) mixed mushrooms, sliced into bite-size pieces, divided

5 tbsp (85g) unsalted butter, divided

1 tsp (3g) salt

1 tsp (3g) black pepper

6 cups (1.5L) chicken stock or vegetable stock

1 tbsp (15ml) olive oil

½ onion, finely diced

1 cup (200g) arborio rice

½ cup (125ml) dry white wine

2 tbsp (30ml) gochujang

1 cup (170g) kimchi, roughly chopped

1 cup (120g) freshly grated Parmesan cheese, divided

Finely sliced green onion, to garnish

Note

Always taste as you cook to check the flavor and doneness of the rice. Save some leftovers for the recipe on the next page.

Scan for bonus content.

Arancini

serves **2–4** | prep **30 minutes** | cook **50 minutes**

The real reason to make risotto is so you have leftovers to make arancini, or as I like to call it, "Italian onigiri." The first time I had it was in Malta, a small island country off the southern coast of Italy. Delicious fried balls of rice with a cheesy center—now who wouldn't love that? Use the leftovers from the Mushroom Kimchi Risotto recipe from the previous page to make this arancini with just a few extra steps.

1 To make the sauce, in a skillet, heat the oil over medium heat. Add the onion and cook for 1 minute. Add the tomato paste and fish sauce, and season with the salt and pepper. Cook for 30 seconds, stirring constantly, and then add the tomatoes and garlic. Cook for 1 minute more, and then add the white wine, mirin, and brown sugar. Bring to a simmer, then reduce the heat to low and cook for 30 minutes more. Remove from heat, and stir in the basil. Set aside.

2 To make the arancini, first prepare your workstation by placing the flour in a small bowl, the eggs in another small bowl, and the panko in a third small bowl. Place a bowl of cold water nearby for wetting your hands.

3 Lightly wet your hands with cold water. Grab a small handful of risotto and use both your hands to form a ball. With your finger, poke a hole into the core of the risotto ball. Insert 1 mozzarella ball and close the hole.

4 Coat the stuffed risotto ball in the flour, then in the egg wash, and then in the panko, making sure it's coated generously in the breadcrumbs. Repeat with the remaining risotto.

5 In a Dutch oven or deep, heavy saucepan, heat the oil over medium heat. Test the temperature of the oil by dropping a small crumb into it. If it starts to sizzle immediately, the oil is ready.

6 Gently place the coated risotto balls into the hot oil, 2 or 3 at a time. Cook for a total of 8 to 10 minutes or until golden brown, making sure to rotate the risotto balls every 2 minutes so they fry evenly. Once cooked, remove from the oil and transfer to a plate lined with paper towel.

7 Serve immediately with the marinara sauce. Garnish with freshly grated Parmesan cheese, if desired.

For the marinara sauce
2 tbsp (30ml) olive oil
¼ yellow onion, diced
2 tbsp (30ml) tomato paste
2 tsp (10ml) fish sauce
1 tsp (3g) salt
1 tsp (3g) black pepper
4 tomatoes, diced
4 garlic cloves, chopped
½ cup (125ml) dry white wine
2 tbsp (30ml) mirin
1 tbsp (15g) brown sugar
Handful of fresh basil leaves, chopped

For the arancini
½ cup (60g) all-purpose flour
2 eggs, lightly beaten
2 cups (120g) panko breadcrumbs
2–4 cups (300–500g) cold leftover Mushroom Kimchi Risotto (page 227)
4–6 mozzarella balls
2 cups (500ml) canola oil
Freshly grated Parmesan cheese, to garnish

Pulled Mushroom
on Grilled Rice Paper

serves **2** | prep **5 minutes** | cook **10 minutes**

Many mushrooms can be shredded like pulled pork, which makes them super versatile in cooking. Once shredded and cooked, they keep a nice, chewy mushroom texture, close to the same mouthfeel as pulled pork. Mushrooms like oysters, chanterelle, chicken of the woods, king trumpet, boletes, and enoki would all work for this dish, which is a version of the popular Vietnamese street food sometimes referred to as "Vietnamese pizza." This is made by grilling rice paper (the same kind used for spring rolls) and mixing in eggs along with various ingredients.

1 In a large, dry skillet over medium heat, sauté the mushrooms for 2 to 5 minutes or until the moisture in the mushrooms has been drawn out and evaporated. Add the butter, fish sauce, and chilis, and cook for 2 to 4 minutes. Remove from the heat and set aside.

2 Preheat a charcoal grill to medium heat or preheat a large skillet on the stovetop.

3 Place 1 sheet of rice paper on the grill, and spread 1 egg yolk over the entire sheet of rice paper. Repeat with the remaining piece of rice paper and egg yolk. Top each piece of rice paper with mushrooms, shallots, peanuts, and green onions. Add sriracha or hot sauce to your liking. Cook for 3 to 5 minutes. The rice paper is cooked once it starts to turn opaque.

4 Serve open-face, like a pizza, or folded over, like a taco.

8oz (225g) fresh mushrooms, shredded

2 tbsp (30g) butter

1 tsp (5ml) fish sauce

½ tsp (1g) minced fresh Thai chilis or chili flakes

2 sheets rice paper

2 egg yolks

2 tbsp (7g) fried shallots

2 tbsp (12g) crushed peanuts

¼ cup (25g) chopped green onion

2 tsp (10ml) sriracha or hot sauce

Mushroom Enchiladas

serves **2** | prep **15 minutes** | cook **20 minutes**

If I had to choose a last meal, these enchiladas would be it. This recipe was created by my partner, Jocelyn, who grew up cooking Mexican cuisine with her mother. This is not the cheesy baked casserole version of enchiladas. Instead, fried corn tortillas are dipped in a homemade tomato salsa, wrapped around savory sautéed wild mushrooms, and topped with crema, cotija, and onion for a fresh and deeply flavorful dish.

1 To make the salsa, heat a large skillet over medium-high heat. Add the whole tomatoes, peppers, onion, and garlic to the dry pan. (This step does not require any oil.) Cook for 8 to 10 minutes, turning occasionally, until charred on all sides. Transfer to a plate and let cool.

2 Meanwhile, return the skillet to the stovetop and heat 1 tablespoon (15ml) canola oil over medium-high heat. Add the mushrooms and cook until golden brown. Season with salt to taste, and then transfer to a bowl and set aside.

3 Wipe out the pan and return it to the stovetop over medium heat. Add the remaining ¼ cup (60ml) canola oil. When the oil is hot, fry the tortillas one at a time for approximately 2 minutes on each side, or until golden. They should have lightly crisp edges but still be pliable. Set the fried tortillas aside on a plate.

4 To finish the salsa, in a blender, combine the charred tomatoes, peppers, onion, and garlic. Blend until smooth or salsa consistency. Season with salt to taste.

5 Transfer the salsa to a saucepan, and bring to a simmer over medium heat. When simmering, reduce the heat to low.

6 Dip a fried tortilla into the simmering salsa, coating it fully, and transfer to a plate. Place a handful of cooked mushrooms on top, and roll up the tortilla. Repeat with the rest of the tortillas, arranging them on a serving plate as they are filled.

7 Pour any remaining salsa over the enchiladas and top with the crema, diced onion, crumbled cotija, and shredded lettuce. Serve immediately.

For the salsa

4 Roma tomatoes
2–3 serrano peppers
¼ white onion
3 garlic cloves, peeled
Salt, to taste

For the enchiladas

1 tbsp (15ml) + ¼ cup (60ml) canola oil, divided
1lb (450g) shredded wild mushrooms (oyster, king trumpet, or chanterelle)
Salt, to taste
Four to six 6-in (15cm) corn tortillas
¼ cup (60ml) crema or sour cream
¼ white onion, diced
2 tbsp (10g) crumbled queso cotija
1 cup (50g) shredded little gem lettuce

Note

Shredded chicken, crab, or shrimp can be used in place of mushrooms for the filling.

Mexican markets carry crema, which is similar to sour cream but runnier and more flavorful.

Acknowledgments

First and foremost, I want to extend my heartfelt thanks to my editor, Alex Rigby, and the rest of the team at DK. For all your ideas and guidance on writing the book, as well as reaching out to me in the first place to offer me this incredible opportunity. Your keen eye and thoughtful feedback transformed my ideas into a cohesive and inspiring collection. Your unwavering support throughout this journey has been invaluable.

To my partner, Jocelyn, thank you for your endless encouragement and love. As the main photographer for this cookbook, you captured each dish with such artistry and passion, bringing my recipes to life in ways I could only dream of. Your patience and enthusiasm kept me motivated, and I am so grateful for the countless moments we shared working on this book. From late night photo shoots to making it work while living out of a van, we made it happen. Only you and I truly know the amount of work it took to bring this to life. I love you!

To one of my best friends, Dwight, for all the amazing artwork. Your stunning gyotaku have added an extraordinary touch to this book, enhancing the visual richness and appeal. May our travels continue each year until we catch every species of fish.

To Matt and Lia, for hosting us every time we're in Alaska and taking us on some of the most memorable trips throughout this whole journey, and then some. As well as for bringing me into Barnacle Foods to be part of creating my first commercially produced product, Kelp Chili Crisp. I hope for the best for your new addition to the family coming soon!

To Steph and Raul, for allowing us to use your home as our home base in the Bay Area to come and go as we please and to have endless packages sent to your address. It would not have been possible to move out of our rental to chase our travel dreams without you guys. Jocelyn and I are always grateful for your generosity.

To my mate Chris in New Zealand, for taking in me and Jocelyn as we experienced what everybody called the worst summer in NZ—filled with rainstorms and floods. Thank you, Callan, Edward, and Arthur, for becoming our host family. Whenever you want to come for a visit to our new property, don't hesitate to say the word!

To Sven, for letting me borrow your beautiful handcrafted ceramics for the photo shoots! Looking forward to taking workshops at your new studio in San Francisco.

To all my friends and family, for the endless support and encouragement. Danny Woo for looking over my writing, Kevin Candido for letting us crash and use your kitchen, and everybody else that helped us along the way!

Lastly, I want to express my deepest gratitude to my subscribers. Your support and enthusiasm for my culinary adventures have been the driving force behind this project. It's your support that made this cookbook possible, and I hope it brings you as much joy as you've given me.

Thank you all for believing in this journey!

Taku Kondo is a popular YouTuber and former sushi chef who sustainably harvests his own ingredients to create masterful dishes. Focusing mainly on fishing and foraging, he specializes in preparing restaurant-quality meals in the great outdoors. Taku lives in Northern California, where he is often on the water or in the woods, seeking his next big catch or mushroom haul. He frequently travels around the globe to expand his knowledge of fishing and cuisines. Follow his outdoor adventures on YouTube, Instagram, and Facebook: @outdoorcheflife.